Green

NATIONAL GEOGRAPHIC LEARNING | WADSWORTH CENGAGE Learning·

Australia • Brazil • Japan • Korea • Mexico • Singapore • Spain • United Kingdom • United States

Green

Publisher: Monica Eckman

Acquiring Sponsoring Editor:
Kate Derrick

Project Manager: John Haley

Subject Matter Expert:
Kathy Kessler, PhD

Assistant Editor: Danielle Warchol

Editorial Assistant: Maggie Cross

Media Editor: Cara Douglass-Graff

Marketing Director:
Lindsey Richardson

Marketing Communications
Manager: Linda Yip

Content Project Manager:
Corinna Dibble

Design Director: Bruce Bond

Manufacturing Planner:
Mary Beth Hennebury

Rights Acquisition Specialist:
Alexandra Ricciardi

Production and composition:
Integra

Text and Cover Designer:
Bruce Bond

Cover Image: David Evans/National
Geographic Image Collection

For product information and technology assistance, contact us at
Cengage Learning Customer & Sales Support, 1-800-354-9706

For permission to use material from this text or product, submit all requests online at **www.cengage.com/permissions.**
Further permissions questions can be emailed to
permissionrequest@cengage.com.

Library of Congress Control Number: 2012933142

ISBN-13: 978-1-133-60358-0
ISBN-10: 1-133-60358-0

Wadsworth
20 Channel Center Street
Boston, MA 02210
USA

Cengage Learning is a leading provider of customized learning solutions with office locations around the globe, including Singapore, the United Kingdom, Australia, Mexico, Brazil and Japan. Locate your local office at
international.cengage.com/region

Cengage Learning products are represented in Canada by Nelson Education, Ltd.

For your course and learning solutions, visit **www.cengage.com.**

Purchase any of our products at your local college store or at our preferred online store **www.cengagebrain.com.**

Instructors: Please visit **login.cengage.com** and log in to access instructor-specific resources.

Printed in Canada
1 2 3 4 5 6 7 16 15 14 13 12

Table *of* Contents

About the Series

Cengage Learning and National Geographic Learning are proud to present the *National Geographic Learning Reader Series*. This ground breaking series is brought to you through an exclusive partnership with the National Geographic Society, an organization that represents a tradition of amazing stories, exceptional research, first-hand accounts of exploration, rich content, and authentic materials.

The series brings learning to life by featuring compelling images, media, and text from National Geographic. Through this engaging content, students develop a clearer understanding of the world around them. Published in a variety of subject areas, the *National Geographic Learning Reader Series* connects key topics in each discipline to authentic examples and can be used in conjunction with most standard texts or online materials available for your courses.

How the reader works

Each article is focused on one topic relevant to the discipline. The introduction provides context to orient students and focus questions that suggest ideas to think about while reading the selection. Rich photography, compelling images, and pertinent maps are amply used to further enhance understanding of the selections. The chapter culminating section includes discussion questions to stimulate both in-class discussion and out-of-class work.

A premium eBook will accompany each reader and will provide access to the text online with a media library that may include images, videos, and other premium content specific to each individual discipline.

National Geographic Learning Readers are currently available in a variety of course areas, including Archeology, Architecture and Construction, Biological Anthropology, Biology, Earth Science, English Composition, Environmental Science, Geography, Geology, Meteorology, Oceanography, and Sustainability.

Few organizations present this world, its people, places, and precious resources in a more compelling way than National Geographic. Through this reader series we honor the mission and tradition of National Geographic Society: to inspire people to care about the planet.

This reader's themes are inspired by our changing relationship with the earth, based on an understanding that the planet's resources are finite and that our future well-being depends on preserving them. While the term *green* signifies a level of awareness about environmental concerns, we use it here in the broadest sense, to draw your attention to the state of the planet and to promote discourse on how to address the needs of the human population as well as the ecosystems that sustain life in our world. To what extent we see ourselves as members of a global community and to rethink how we will meet the growing needs of our population in the future are two central questions this collection asks readers to consider critically.

This National Geographic reader examines a range of topics relating to the human footprint, which has begun to raise unprecedented global concerns. Barbara Kingsolver's "Fresh Water" begins the collection and serves as a centerpiece, offering insights on water, perhaps our most precious resource. It is seen here as a symbol and as a literal measure of climate change, "the visible face of climate." While global warming comes up in various ways throughout the readings, it remains an important thread rather than an independent theme. Conversely, water, in its many forms, represents a fundamental theme, viewed as a basic and dwindling resource in "Water Pressure" and "The Drying of the West" and as a force held precariously within glacial ice. "The Big Melt" addresses some consequences of a warming planet that are already being felt throughout Asia.

Several of the essays that appear here take a fresh look at our natural resources and their value, not only as sources of marketable products, but also in terms of their environmental worth. As consumers of food, fuel, and timber, and as producers of carbon dioxide and toxic waste, our sheer numbers have profoundly changed the balance upon which the environment and perhaps our own future depend. Can we restore that balance and adopt sustainable approaches? "The End of Plenty" asks readers to consider a human population struggling to find enough food while the world's corn harvests feed livestock and ethanol production. And while high-tech fishing—made profitable by the demands of wealthier nations—has depleted the world's oceans for all ("The Global Fish Crisis"), the international market for beef and soy provide powerful incentive to destroy what remains of the world's largest rainforest in order to plant crops and raise cattle ("Last of the Amazon"). Recognizing that our own heritage as well as our environmental integrity is tied to our redwood forests, J. Michael Fay examines what it would take to restore the last remnants of a uniquely American ecosystem in "The Redwoods Point the Way."

If water is the source of life, energy consumption and the demand for fuel have become hallmarks of life in our technology-driven and industrialized world. While the potential for long-term devastation related to climate change is no longer in question, the demand for energy continues to grow. "The 21st Century Grid" and "Saving Energy: It Starts at Home" explore our energy use and some steps we can take as nations and as individuals to eliminate waste, increase efficiency, and reduce our carbon emissions. But as we develop new technology and upgrade our electronic devices, where does our toxic e-waste go? "High-Tech Trash" answers that question and offers compelling reasons for us to find ways to responsibly dispose of computers, televisions, and cell phones. Finally, what direction will a commitment to clean energy take? Do we have the ability to learn from mistakes ("The Gulf of Oil: The Deep Dilemma") and invest wisely in renewable energy ("Can Solar Save Us?")? Collectively, the readings included here ask us to consider the cost of not doing so.

FRESH WATER

Barbara Kingsolver's reflective essay holds a special place in this reader, not only because it draws a connection between the personal view of this essential element of life and a global view, but also because it asks us to examine more deeply what water means to us as individuals.

As you read "Fresh Water," consider the following questions:

- How does seeing water as "the visible face of climate" work to give us perspective on water's role in our planet?
- How might this extend to our relationship with other resources?

FRESH
WATER

During a 1972 drought in Bangladesh, a farmer dispensed precious water plant by plant.

THE AMOUNT OF MOISTURE ON EARTH HAS NOT CHANGED. THE WATER THE DINOSAURS DRANK MILLIONS OF YEARS AGO IS THE SAME WATER THAT FALLS AS RAIN TODAY. BUT WILL THERE BE ENOUGH FOR A MORE CROWDED WORLD?

We keep an eye out for wonders, my daughter and I, every morning as we walk down our farm lane to meet the school bus. And wherever we find them, they reflect the magic of water: a spider web drooping with dew like a rhinestone necklace. A rain-colored heron rising from the creek bank. One astonishing morning, we had a visitation of frogs. Dozens of them hurtled up from the grass ahead of our feet, launching themselves, white-bellied, in bouncing arcs, as if we'd been caught in a downpour of amphibians. It seemed to mark the dawning of some new aqueous age. On another day we met a snapping turtle in his primordial olive drab armor. Normally this is a pond-locked creature, but some murky ambition had moved him onto our gravel lane, using the rainy week as a passport from our farm to somewhere else.

The little, nameless creek tumbling through our hollow holds us in thrall. Before we came to southern Appalachia, we lived for years in Arizona, where a permanent runnel of that size would merit a nature preserve. In

> The **morality of an act** is a function of the state of the system at the time it is performed.

the Grand Canyon State, every license plate reminded us that water changes the face of the land, splitting open rock desert like a peach, leaving mile-deep gashes of infinite hue. Cities there function like space stations, importing every ounce of fresh water from distant rivers or fossil aquifers. But such is the human inclination to take water as a birthright that public fountains still may bubble in Arizona's town squares and farmers there raise thirsty crops. Retirees from rainier climes irrigate green lawns that impersonate the grasslands they left behind. The truth encroaches on all the fantasies, though, when desert residents wait months between rains, watching cacti tighten their belts and roadrunners skirmish over precious beads from a dripping garden faucet. Water is life. It's the briny broth of our origins, the pounding circulatory system of the world, a precarious molecular edge on which we survive. It makes up two-thirds of our bodies, just like the map

Adapted from "Fresh Water" by Barbara Kingsolver: National Geographic Magazine, April 2010.

of the world; our vital fluids are saline, like the ocean. The apple doesn't fall far from the tree.

Even while we take Mother Water for granted, humans understand in our bones that she is the boss. We stake our civilizations on the coasts and mighty rivers. Our deepest dread is the threat of having too little moisture—or too much. We've lately raised the Earth's average temperature by .74°C (1.3°F), a number that sounds inconsequential. But these words do not: flood, drought, hurricane, rising sea levels, bursting levees. Water is the visible face of climate and, therefore, climate change. Shifting rain patterns flood some regions and dry up others as nature demonstrates a grave physics lesson: Hot air holds more water molecules than cold.

The results are in plain sight along pummeled coasts from Louisiana to the Philippines as superwarmed air above the ocean brews superstorms, the likes of which we have never known. In arid places the same physics amplify evaporation and drought, visible in the dust-dry farms of the Murray-Darling River Basin in Australia. On top of the Himalaya, glaciers whose meltwater sustains vast populations are dwindling. The snapping turtle I met on my lane may have been looking for higher ground. Last summer brought us a string of floods that left tomatoes blighted on the vine and our farmers needing disaster relief for the third consecutive year. The past decade has brought us more extreme storms than ever before, of the kind that dump many inches in a day, laying down crops and utility poles and great sodden oaks whose roots cannot find purchase in the saturated ground. The word "disaster" seems to mock us. After enough repetitions of shocking weather, we can't remain indefinitely shocked.

Our trust in Earth's infinite generosity was half right, as every raindrop will run to the ocean, and the ocean will rise into the firmament.

How can the world shift beneath our feet? All we know is founded on its rhythms: Water will flow from the snow-capped mountains, rain and sun will arrive in their proper seasons. Humans first formed our tongues around language, surely, for the purpose of explaining these constants to our children. What should we tell them now? That "reliable" has been rained out, or died of thirst? When the Earth seems to raise its own voice to the pitch of a gale, have we the ears to listen?

A world away from my damp hollow, the Bajo Piura Valley is a great bowl of the driest Holocene sands I've ever gotten in my shoes. Stretching from coastal, northwestern Peru into southern Ecuador, the 14,000-square-mile Piura Desert is home to many endemic forms of thorny life. Profiles of this eco-region describe it as dry to drier, and Bajo Piura on its southern edge is what anyone would call driest. Between January and March it might get close to an inch of rain, depending on the whims of El Niño, my driver explained as we bumped over the dry bed of the Río Piura, "but in some years, nothing at all." For hours we passed through white-crusted fields ruined by years of irrigation and then into eye-burning valleys beyond the limits of endurance for anything but sparse stands of the deep-rooted *Prosopis pallida,* arguably nature's most arid-adapted tree. And remarkably, some scattered families of *Homo sapiens.*

They are economic refugees, looking for land that costs nothing. In Bajo Piura they find it, although living there has other costs, and fragile drylands pay their own price too, as people exacerbate desertification by cutting anything living for firewood. What brought me there, as a journalist, was an innovative reforestation project. Peruvian conservationists, partnered with the NGO Heifer International, were guiding the population into herding goats, which eat the protein-rich pods of the native mesquite and disperse its seeds over the desert. In the shade of a stick shelter, a young mother set her dented pot on a dung-fed fire and showed how she curdles goat's milk into white cheese. But milking goats is hard to work into her schedule when she, and every other woman she knows, must walk about eight hours a day to collect water.

Their husbands were digging a well nearby. They worked with hand trowels, a plywood form for lining the shaft with concrete, inch by inch, and a sturdy hand-built crank for lowering a man to the bottom and sending up buckets of sand. A dozen hopeful men in stained straw hats stood back to let me inspect their work, which so far had yielded only a mountain of exhumed sand, dry as dust. I looked down that black hole, then turned and climbed the sand mound to hide my unprofessional tears. I could not fathom this kind of perseverance and wondered how long these beleaguered people would last before they'd had enough of their water woes and moved somewhere else.

Five years later they are still bringing up dry sand, scratching out their fate as a microcosm of life on this planet. There is nowhere else. Forty percent of the households in sub-Saharan Africa are more than a half hour from the nearest water, and that distance is growing. Australian farmers can't follow the rainfall patterns that have shifted south to fall on the sea. A salmon that runs into a dam when homing in on her natal stream cannot make other plans. Together we dig in, for all we're worth.

Since childhood I've heard it's possible to look up from the bottom of a well and see stars, even in daylight. Aristotle wrote about this, and so did Charles Dickens. On many a dark night the vision of that round slip of sky with stars has comforted me. Here's the only problem: It's not true. Western civilization was in no great hurry to give up this folklore; astronomers believed it for centuries, but a few of them eventually thought to test it and had their illusions dashed by simple observation.

Civilization has been similarly slow to give up on our myth of the Earth's infinite generosity. Declining to look for evidence to the contrary, we just knew it was there. We pumped aquifers and diverted rivers, trusting the twin lucky stars of unrestrained human expansion and endless supply. Now water tables plummet in countries harboring half the world's population. Rather grandly, we have overdrawn our accounts.

In 1968 the ecologist Garrett Hardin wrote a paper called "The Tragedy of the Commons," required reading for biology students ever since. It addresses the problems that can be solved only by "a change in human values or ideas of morality" in situations where rational pursuit of individual self-interest leads to collective ruin. Cattle farmers who share a common pasture, for example, will increase their herds one by one until they destroy the pasture by overgrazing. Agreeing to self-imposed limits instead, unthinkable at first, will become the right thing to do. While our laws imply that morality is fixed, Hardin made the point that "the morality of an act is a function of the state of the system at the time it is performed." Surely it was no sin, once upon a time, to shoot and make pies of passenger pigeons.

Water is the ultimate commons. Watercourses once seemed as boundless as those pigeons that darkened the sky overhead, and the notion of protecting water was as silly as bottling it. But rules change. Time and again, from New Mexico's antique irrigation codes to the UN Convention on International Watercourses, communities have studied water systems and redefined wise use. Now Ecuador has become the first nation on Earth to put the rights of nature in its constitution so that rivers and forests are not simply property but maintain their own right to flourish. Under these laws a citizen might file suit on behalf of an injured watershed, recognizing that its health is crucial to the common good. Other nations may follow Ecuador's lead. Just as legal systems once reeled to comprehend women or former slaves as fully entitled, law schools in the United States are now reforming their curricula with an eye to understanding and acknowledging nature's rights.

On my desk, a glass of water has caught the afternoon light, and I'm still looking for wonders. Who owns this water? How can I call it mine when its fate is to run through rivers and living bodies, so many already and so many more to come? It is an ancient, dazzling relic, temporarily quarantined here in my glass, waiting to return to its kind, waiting to move a mountain. It is the gold standard of biological currency, and the good news is that we can conserve it in countless ways. Also, unlike petroleum, water will always be with us. Our trust in Earth's infinite generosity was half right, as every raindrop will run to the ocean, and the ocean will rise into the firmament. And half wrong, because we are not important to water. It's the other way around. Our task is to work out reasonable ways to survive inside its boundaries. We'd be wise to fix our sights on some new stars. The gentle nudge of evidence, the guidance of science, and a heart for protecting the commons: These are the tools of a new century. Taking a wide-eyed look at a watery planet is our way of knowing the stakes, the better to know our place.

Discussion Questions

- What effect does Kingsolver's use of figurative language have on the reader?

- What purpose does the name "Mother Water" serve in this essay?

- How does the author's tone reinforce her message?

- How does the Bajo Piura Valley example point to larger issues related to climate change?

Writing Activities

- Write a reflective essay that describes your relationship with water, how you experience it, value it, and take it for granted. Based on your reflections, what does water mean to you, and why? Make sure to explain how Kingsolver's observations may have inspired you to think differently about water's role in your life, and how we think about it.

- In what ways are the "beleaguered people" described in the essay a "microcosm of life on this planet?" Taking Kingsolver's examples as a starting point, write an essay that explains how we are all tied to water, and how in some ways water ties us together.

- What is the author's purpose in including the myth of the stars and "the myth of the earth's infinite generosity"? Write an essay that explains what the author's reference to these two myths says about us, our assumptions, and our current situation.

- Write an essay that examines the idea that changing circumstances demand changing laws. Explain this concept by examining how it relates to conservation, agriculture, renewable resources, energy consumption, or any other issue that you see directly connected to the state of the planet. Focus on one or two issues that seem important to you.

Collaborative Activities

- With a partner or two, discuss the meaning of the statement "water is the ultimate commons." Consolidate your ideas and share them with the class or with another group.

- Working in a small group, examine the observations Kingsolver makes in the last paragraph. Why are they important? What is she asking us to consider here?

LAST OF THE AMAZON

Saving the Amazonian rain forest has been one of the most widely publicized environmental issues, beginning decades before concerns about global warming captured the world's attention. Scott Wallace's 2007 article illustrates how new threats have taken hold, resulting in a continuing battle for land and for profit in a region where death can sometimes be the price of defending the remaining forest.

As you read "Last of the Amazon," consider the following questions:

- What factors contribute to rainforest destruction and how have new challenges developed despite ongoing environmental concerns?
- What roles do market demands play in perpetuating land fraud and other types of corruption in the region?

At current clearing rates, and with climate change continuing, scientists predict that 40 percent of the Amazon will be destroyed and a further 20 percent degraded within two decades.

LAST OF THE
AMAZON

Remnant patches of Brazilian rain forest, the world's most biologically diverse habitat, edge land chainsawed, bulldozed, and scorched to make way for crops and cattle.

IN THE TIME IT TAKES TO READ THIS ARTICLE, AN AREA OF BRAZIL'S RAIN FOREST LARGER THAN 200 FOOTBALL FIELDS WILL HAVE BEEN DESTROYED.

Scientists fear that an additional **20 percent of the trees will be lost over the next two decades.**

The market forces of globalization are invading the Amazon, hastening the demise of the forest and thwarting its most committed stewards. In the past three decades, hundreds of people have died in land wars; countless others endure fear and uncertainly, their lives threatened by those who profit from the theft of timber and land. In this Wild West frontier of guns, chain saws, and bulldozers, government agents are often corrupt and ineffective—or ill-equipped and outmatched. Now, industrial-scale soybean producers are joining loggers and cattle ranchers in the land grab, speeding up destruction and further fragmenting the great Brazilian wilderness.

During the past 40 years, close to 20 percent of the Amazon rain forest has been cut down—more than in all the previous 450 years since European colonization began. The percentage could well be far higher; the figure fails to account for selective logging, which causes significant damage but is less easily observable than clear-cuts. Scientists fear that an additional 20 percent of the trees will be lost over the next two decades. If that happens, the forest's ecology will begin to unravel. Intact, the Amazon produces half its own rainfall through the moisture it releases into the atmosphere. Eliminate enough of that rain through clearing, and the remaining trees dry out and die. When desiccation is worsened by global warming, severe droughts raise the specter of wildfires that could ravage the forest. Such a drought afflicted the Amazon in 2005, reducing river levels as much as 40 feet and stranding hundreds of communities. Meanwhile, because trees are being wantonly burned to create open land in the frontier states of Pará, Mato Grosso, Acre, and Rondônia, Brazil has become one of the world's largest emitters of greenhouse gases. The danger signs are undeniable.

Adapted from "Last of the Amazon" by Scott Wallace: National Geographic Magazine, January 2007.

A boy mourns activist Dorothy Stang at a gathering to mark the first anniversary of her murder. The 73-year-old nun, who dedicated her life to saving the forest and helping workers, was killed by hired gunmen in 2005 after trying to stop ranchers from clearing land. White crosses represent 772 victims of land wars in the state of Pará, and 48 red crosses symbolize local people now under death threats.

All of it starts with a road. Except for a handful of federal and state highways—including the east-west Trans-Amazon Highway and the controversial BR-163, the "soy highway," which splits the heart of the Amazon along 1,100 miles from southern Mato Grosso north to Santarém in Pará—nearly every road in the Amazon is unauthorized. There are more than 105,000 miles of these roads, most made illegally by loggers to reach mahogany and other hardwoods for the lucrative export market.

In Brazil, the events set in motion by logging are almost always more destructive than the logging itself. Once the trees are extracted and the loggers have moved on, the roads serve as conduits for an explosive mix of squatters, speculators, ranchers, farmers, and, invariably, hired gunmen. The land sharks follow the roads deep into previously impenetrable forest, then destroy tracts to make it look as if they own them. Land thievery is committed through corruption, strong-arm tactics, and fraudulent titles and is so widespread that Brazilians have a name for it: *grilagem,* from the Portuguese word *grilo,* or cricket. *Grileiros,* the practitioners, have been known to age phony land titles in a drawer full of hungry crickets. When Brazil's agrarian reform agency, Instituto Nacional de Colonização e Reforma Agrária, reviewed

Amazonian land ownership records over the past three years, it voided more than 62,000 claims that appeared to be fraudulent.

Guarantã do Norte, a city of 32,000 at the northern extremity of the paved section of BR-163, is the regional headquarters of Brazil's environmental protection agency, Instituto Brasileiro do Meio Ambiente e dos Recursos Naturals Renováveis (IBAMA), With only a handful of inspectors to monitor thousands of square miles of territory, Márcio da Costa, the 1BAMA chief, is overwhelmed, He works from a makeshift office behind the charred wreckage of the former headquarters, which was torched by an angry mob in 2004 after IBAMA agents and police broke a ring of timber traffickers, shutting down illegal sawmills and issuing millions of dollars in fines to loggers in the nearby town of Alta Floresta. The inquest into the arson failed to produce a single suspect.

A sputtering air conditioner barely churned the soupy air as da Costa showed me a 2004 logging certificate, along with a carbon copy. The copy, signed by an export inspector 1,500 miles away in southern Brazil, listed thousands of cubic feet of wood nowhere to be found on the original document—all contraband. "Yesterday, we seized five trucks loaded with, timber coming out of the same area," da Costa said.

In 2005, after gunmen hired by grileiros murdered Sister Dorothy Stang, a U.S.-born nun and environmental activist, the Brazilian government accelerated a crackdown, suspending logging permits throughout the Amazon—most of which had been falsified to launder illegal timber. Federal police and IBAMA intensified their investigation into irregularities in the timber business. Waves of troops were dispatched to Mato Grosso and Pará. They seized truckload after truckload of contraband timber. Of the more than 300 people arrested, about 100 turned out to be IBAMA officials involved in a far-reaching conspiracy to sell millions of cubic feet of endangered hardwoods to the United States, Europe, and Asia.

To reduce fraud, Brazil will soon introduce electronic logging certificates. Meanwhile, to aid in policing the sprawling Amazon hinterland, government agents are turning to satellite technology and remote sensing to alert them to the work of grileiros. Yet even when officials spot *a desmatamento,* or illegal clearing, they are usually hamstrung by a lack of manpower or equipment. And when the police do react, the resources they manage to scrape together can be modest.

Such was the experience of José Rosa, a rancher in the frontier town of Matupá, 20 miles south of Guarantã do Norte, who had discovered that grileiros were cutting trees on his property. It's not that Rosa objected to the idea of clearing land—he himself plans to plant 2,500 acres in the coming year—it's just that someone else was blatantly trying to steal his. Despite federal pledges for more resources to combat timber mafias and land sharks, the only help Rosa could round up was a tiny posse of two IBAMA agents and a local cop. Among them, they carried a single pistol and a pump-action shotgun—not much of an arsenal against heavily armed grileiros. To buy gasoline for their pickup truck, the IBAMA agents had to dig into their own pockets.

On his property, we headed uphill through fenced-off pasture and entered the darkness of the forest along a two-rut road made by grileiros. We crossed a stream, so clear and inviting that we stopped for a drink. As I beheld the green cathedral that towered above us, I had the sense that we were day-tripping in a sacred place that should have taken weeks of arduous trekking to reach. An iridescent blue morpho butterfly lilted past, one of a million wonders still harbored by this primal forest. But for how much longer? Recalling the murky stew I'd seen in streams already, overrun by farmland farther south, I figured it would be only months—not even a year—before these deep, mysterious shadows were exposed to scorching sunlight and the cool, clean water no longer fit to drink.

Bouncing along washed-out tire tracks overhung by low branches, we suddenly emerged onto a wider, newly graded road, "These aren't poor people doing this," Rosa said, "These are land grabbers. They have a lot of money. If they find me out here alone, they will kill me."

The Amazon land rush has its roots in the 1970s, when Brazil's military dicta-

These aren't poor people doing this. These are land grabbers. They have a lot of money. If they find me out here alone, they will kill me.

torship pursued a policy of *"integrar para não entregar,"* meaning "occupy it or risk losing it." Destitute settlers followed the central axes of penetration, the Trans-Amazon and BR-163, into the jungle, escaping poverty in Brazil's overcrowded south and northeast. Many perished or gave up, but others survived and adapted to the harsh life, practicing slash-and-burn farming.

The poorest settlers were rarely given title to the land they worked, but the government awarded concessions to the well connected—blocks of up to 7,400 acres—to encourage logging, ranching, and other development. If grantees (usually absentee landlords) failed to put the land to productive use within five years, they would forfeit the right to permanent ownerships and control was to revert to

WORLD DEMAND FOR BRAZIL'S PRODUCTS

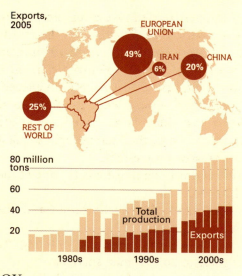

SOY
Soybean production in the Brazilian Amazon soared after heat-tolerant varieties were introduced in 1997. Brazil may soon lead the world in soybeans, surpassing the United States.

SOURCE: ECONOMIC RESEARCH SERVICE USDA

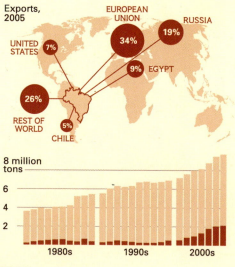

BEEF
The world's largest exporter of beef since 2004, Brazil now supplies nearly every country, including emerging markets such as Algeria, Romania, and Egypt.

the federal government. Most grantees did nothing but still considered themselves the rightful owners. Meanwhile, landless squatters moved in from adjacent lots, working plots "whose ownership the government failed to resolve. That has fueled a bloody showdown pitting the powerful absentee elites who raze forest for agribusiness against family farmers who clear small patches for crops but still depend on intact forest around them for survival.

"What's happening today in Amazonia is a clash between two models of development," said Felicio Pontes, one of a new breed of government lawyers seeking to prosecute corruption, land fraud, and environmental crimes in the Amazon. We were standing in a mock cemetery of 820 crosses that symbolized the human cost of the land wars in Pará, on the first anniversary of the murder of Dorothy Stang. "The first model was implanted during the military dictatorship, based on timber extraction and cattle. It's predatory because it causes death, it's not renewable, and it devastates the forest." The alternative model, preached by Stang, is what Pontes calls social environmentalism. The first concentrates wealth, the second calls for its dispersion in small-scale agroforestry collectives.

Dorothy Stang, born and raised in Ohio, a sister of Notre Dame de Namur, was revered for her dedication to the ideal of family farmers who extract their sustenance in harmony with the forest. From her base in the frontier town of Anapu, she worked unceasingly to transform settlers along the Trans-Amazon Highway into environmentally conscious, cohesive, and combative communities, able to resist violent cliques of ranchers and speculators who would lay claim to the same land. Stang saw human rights and environmental conservation in the Amazon as inextricably intertwined. Though poor settlers themselves damage the forest, Stang believed they could learn to manage their land sustainably as a matter of self-preservation. "The death of the forest is the end of our lives," she told her followers.

Her last mission, to save a remote tract of jungle known as Lot 55, ended on the morning of February 12, 2005, when two gunmen confronted the petite 73-year-old nun on a secluded jungle path. A conversation ensued, overheard by a witness who later testified at the men's trial. Stang admonished them—the land was not theirs, they had no right to plant pasture grasses for livestock.

"So, you don't like to eat meat?" one of the assailants taunted.

"Not enough to destroy the forest for it," she replied.

"If this problem isn't resolved today, it's never going to be," the man snarled.

Stang saw him reach for his gun. She opened her Bible to Matthew and read from chapter five, "*Bem-aventurados as que têm fome e sede de justiça, pois serão satisfeitos*—Blessed are they who hunger and thirst for justice, for they shall be satisfied." As she turned to go,

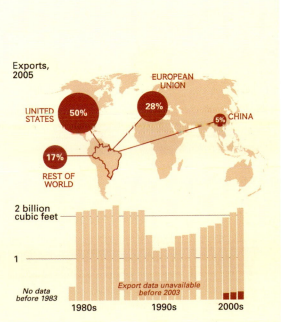

TIMBER

Demand for Brazilian hardwoods in Europe, the United States, and Asia has been growing in recent years. Most timber from the Amazon Basin is taken illegally and stays in Brazil.

Rayfrán das Neves Sales leveled his revolver and squeezed the trigger.

Blairo Maggi, governor of the state of Mato Grosso, is seen by the environmental movement as the poster boy for predation. Maggi is "O Rei da Soja," King of Soy, the world's largest single producer. Maggi acquired a less flattering honorific when Greenpeace gave him its Golden Chain Saw award in 2005, Mato Grosso having led Brazil in Amazon deforestation for the third straight year, coinciding with his first three years in the governor's palace.

Besides growing soy, corn, and cotton on three gigantic ranches and several smaller ones—almost a million acres in all—Maggi extends credit to and buys soy from some 900 midsize growers. His company, the Maggi Group, built an entire city, Sapezal, in western Mato Grosso to service a single plantation. And rather than waiting for the federal government to pave BR-163 all the way to the Amazon River at Santarém for transshipment of soy overseas, the Maggi Group created an infrastructure of silos, tugs, and barges to store and transport it down the Madeira River to its own deepwater port at Itacoatiara.

Blairo Maggi's fortunes have paralleled Brazil's accelerating deforestation and emergence as a global agricultural powerhouse. The country is the world leader in beef exports and second only to the United States in soybeans. "The only place left for serious expansion of soy is Brazil," says Oswaldo de Carvalho, a biologist with the Amazon Environmental Research Institute (IPAM). That means more trees will fall in Pará and Mato Grosso.

To Maggi, deforestation is an overblown issue, a "phobia" that plagues people who can't grasp the enormity of the Amazon. "All of Europe could fit inside the Amazon," he says, "and we'd still have room for two Englands."

What does he think of Dorothy Stang's vision of small growers carrying out sustainable projects in harmony with the land? "Totalmente errado—Completely wrong," Maggi says, adding that without heavy subsidies, such projects ran counter to the march of history and are doomed to failure. "All business tends toward concentration, Unit prices fall, and you need huge volumes to survive."

Not all environmentalists see Maggi in unqualified negative light. "He has seen the wisdom of doing things right on private property as he tries to position Mato Grosso as a world economic superpower," says Dan Nepstad of the Woods Hole Research Center in Massachusetts. The center, together with IPAM, its Brazilian counterpart, is conducting research at Maggi's 202,000-acre Tanguro Ranch, located in the headwaters of the Xingu River. One of their experiments involves assessing the ability of mulch made from microbe-rich rain forest leaf litter to regenerate soil depleted by years of monoculture and ranching. With prodding from Nepstad and others, Maggi supports proposals to certify soy grown by internationally accepted environmental and social standards—standards yet to be written. Maggi has already imposed conditions on his growers: no illegally cleared land, no slave labor, no spraying of agrotoxins within 500 meters of a stream. "There is potential for a win-win situation," says Nepstad, who believes that three-way partnerships among NGOs, the government, and the private sector offer the best hope for stopping rampant clearing.

"We're very responsible environmentally and socially," Maggi said, as we began a tour of Tanguro. "Everything we're doing is aboveboard and within the law." He pointed proudly to the ranch's gleaming cafeteria and the spotlessness of the grounds. "Look around," he said, "you won't find a single scrap of plastic here." Motioning to a barnlike structure that stored herbicides and pesticides, he said, "We keep all our agrotoxins properly ventilated until use."

In a steady rain, our vehicle fishtailing in the mud, we approached a denuded gully straddling a narrow stream; a closer look revealed hundreds of saplings. "When we bought this property," Maggi said, "this riverbank was totally stripped. Now we're regenerating the area."

We continued on a service road, straight as a ruler, along the edge of a mile-long field of yellow-green soy. On one side, row after row of calf-high bushes presented a perfect scene of modern mechanized agriculture. A casual observer might have marveled at the bright green luster of the plants, unaware of the toxic mix required to achieve that sheen. Soybeans need large amounts of acid-neutralizing lime, as well as fertilizers, pesticides, and herbicides. From scientists to native villagers, nearly everyone but Maggi spoke to me with alarm about toxins seeping into the watershed. Indian communities such as the Enawenê-Nawê in Mato Grosso complain of poisoned water and dying fish.

Maggi does not perceive any ill effects from soybean cultivation. "It's environmentally beneficial," he said, looking me straight in the eye. "The land here is very poor. If you don't take the right corrective measures, you couldn't produce anything. It's not true that soy degrades the soil. On the contrary, it puts into the soil what naturally isn't there. Afterward, you can grow anything you want." Researchers agree that proper management of soy fields can increase soil productivity. But in reality, no one knows for sure how long the thin, highly acidic Amazon soils can be propped up, raising the possibility of an eventual two-headed catastrophe: environmental and economic.

On the other side of the service road, a line of magnificent 100-foot-high trees draped in lianas—the very core of an ancient primeval forest—was starkly revealed in cross section.

> **P**eople have to believe **breaking the law** has consequences.

Such vistas of geometric fields carved from virgin jungle have become commonplace in Para and Mato Grosso as the soy frontier advances. While many of the incursions are illegal, many are not. Farmers are entitled to clear up to 20 percent of their land, as long as they maintain the other 80 percent as a so-called legal reserve. If the vegetation on their land is "transitional"— somewhere between rain forest and savanna— they're allowed to clear 50 percent. But laws are only as good as the will to enforce them. "Satellite imagery shows that in many frontier zones there is nearly zero compliance," says Stephan Schwartzman of Environmental Defense, a U.S.-based NGO. "People have to believe breaking the law has consequences."

It appears that landowners are starting to believe it. In the crackdown since Stang's murder, farmers who have cleared more forest than their legal limit have been looking for ways to legitimize their holdings. Sympathetic to their situation, Governor Maggi is allowing them to buy up tracts of non-contiguous forest to comply with the legal reserve statute. He promises stiff fines for violators, but he enforces the law reluctantly. "Brazilian producers are the only ones in the world who are obliged to maintain a reserve," Maggi said. "There should be a royalty for leaving those areas intact—they need to be compensated in some way."

Brazilians are not the only people profiting from soybeans. Along the 500-mile paved stretch of BR-163 between Cuiabá and Guarantã do Norte, there are no fewer than five John Deere dealerships. And at harvest time, fleets of the trademark green-and-yellow combines rumble across the fields flanking the highway, pouring rivers of golden soy into open-bed trucks bound for shiny new silos belonging to ADM, Bunge, and Cargill—all U.S. multinationals.

Because BR-163 is not yet paved to the Amazon River, most of Mato Grosso's soy still leaves the state in diesel-belching convoys that must ply 1,200 treacherous miles to Brazil's congested southern ports. In 2003, when the government announced plans to lay asphalt on the last 650 miles of BR-163 from Guarantã do Norte to Santarém, a frenzied land grab ensued. The scale of devastation forced officials to suspend the paving until they could formulate a forest-management strategy for the region. That plan was unveiled in February 2006, one year after the death of Sister Dorothy Stang, when President Luiz Inácio Lula da Silva announced the protection of 16 million acres of rain forest on the western flank of BR-163 between Guarantã and Santarém. (This is nowhere near Lot 55, the patch of forest Stang died defending, where grileiros are still felling trees.) Within the protected area, companies deemed environmentally responsible will be given limited logging concessions, but no clear-cuts or settlements will be allowed.

The new district adds to an expanded mosaic of parks, reserves, and conservation units that, together with indigenous territories, forms the bulwark of defense against the expansion of the frontier in the central Amazon. These measures may be paying off. Deforestation rates fell more than 30 percent in 2005, and preliminary numbers for 2006 are also down. Indian lands in the Xingu watershed are proving an especially effective barrier. There, militant Kayapó and Panará warriors armed with clubs and shotguns patrol their borders using satellite images furnished by international NGOs to pinpoint illegal clearing, As Stephan Schwartzman puts it: "Where Indian land begins is where deforestation ends."

But Brazil's measures to protect the Amazon must be weighed against its other ambitions. These include plans to build seven dams on the environmentally sensitive Xingu and Madeira Rivers, as well as roads, power lines, oil and gas pipelines, and large-scale mining and industrial projects. The dams will power aluminum smelters, and shipping channels will facilitate river transport of exports to Chinese markets. The dams will also flood millions of acres of forest, releasing methane and other greenhouse gases, destroying biodiversity, and forcing indigenous communities to flee ancestral lands.

As indigenous people intuitively grasp, the benefits the Amazon provides are of incalculable worth: Water cycling, (the forest produces not only half its own rainfall but much of the rain south of the Amazon and east of the Andes), carbon sequestering (by holding and absorbing carbon dioxide, the forest mitigates global warming and cleanses the atmosphere), and maintenance of an unmatched panoply of life. But the marketplace has yet to assign value to the forest: It's far more profitable to cut it down for grazing and farming than to leave it standing. "Tropical deforestation is a classic example of market failure," Schwartzman says. Oddly enough, Maggi would probably agree with Schwartzman's solution: "It's urgent to find mechanisms to compensate forest peoples, and their governments, for the ecosystem services their forests provide."

For Cargill, a Minnesota-based food conglomerate, the greatest urgency lies in getting soybeans to market as cheaply as possible. Anticipating the eventual completion of BR-163, Cargill opened a warehouse and deepwater port in Santarém in 2003. Until it can transport soy there by road, Cargill, like Maggi, has been moving much of it by barge via the Madeira River. "We've exported close to two million tons," Douglas Odoni, the plant's operation manager, told me with pride. We stood on a catwalk above the Cypriot-flagged freighter *Evdoxos* as a giant nozzle disgorged soybeans into

the vessel's belly at the rate of 1,350 tons an hour. Within two weeks, the *Evdoxos* would dock in Amsterdam and unload 52,000 tons of Brazilian soybeans at a crush plant that makes oil and animal feed. "They buy only from us," Odoni yelled above the din of the machinery.

Cargill's operations in the Amazon have been controversial from the start. Federal prosecutors are suing the company over its alleged failure to provide an adequate environmental impact study of the port. Cargill's installation of a soybean washer and dryer has infuriated forest defenders, whose protests have repeatedly closed down the plant. To avoid spoilage, soybeans must be cleaned before they're transported, and for farmers around Santarém, it was only after the

arrival of the washer and dryer that they had a buyer for soy and an incentive to grow it. Deforestation in the area has soared. "Maybe it's true that if Cargill weren't here, they wouldn't plant soy," Odoni conceded. But "if they couldn't sell soybeans to us, there would be no taxes and revenues for the local community."

Last summer, Cargill and Brazil's other big soy traders agreed to a two-year moratorium on buying soy grown on newly deforested land in the Amazon. The agreement is sending a signal to soy producers that the environmental impact of their operations is increasingly important in the world marketplace.

For many in the community of Belterra, an hour's drive south of Santarém, the moratorium comes too late. As the head of the Rural Workers Union local, Auricelia Núnes, 33, represents some 5,000 farming families. These people, she said, had been coaxing a decent living from their small plots, when, in the late 1990s, outsiders from southern Brazil began buying up property for a pittance. "There are many small farmers who don't know the value of money," Núnes said. "They thought the money would last, but it doesn't." Now they languish in Santarém's growing slums.

Those who refused to sell found themselves encircled by an encroaching wasteland, as whining chain saws and raging fires consumed the trees right up to the edge of their land. Their yards were overrun with vipers, bees, and rodents escaping the apocalypse, and when tractors began spraying the cleared fields, toxic clouds of pesticides drifted inio their homes. "Their health was in jeopardy," Núnes said." Many started getting sick. Their animals started dying."

Núnes and her husband, Everaldo Pimentel, still live as traditional family farmers, growing corn, squash, and beans and raising livestock on their 70-acre plot. But Pimentel wanted to show me another place, 15 minutes away by car. We followed yet another dirt road past miles of soy before turning onto a narrower track that traced the edge of a freshly plowed field—the driveway to the farmhouse his grandfather had built in the shade of a large mango tree. This, Pimentel said, was where he had grown up. Four years ago, his father sold the farm to a stranger. Workmen immediately cut down every tree. "In 30 seconds," he said, "they can cause more devastation than a small farmer who's been on the land for 30 years."

Discussion Questions

- How does the contrast between Sister Dorothy Stang and Mato Grosso's governor, Blairo Maggi, shed light on the central issues surrounding efforts to save what remains of the rainforest in Brazil?

- Examine Maggi's claims about being "very responsible environmentally and socially" (18). Does the researchers' view of him as part of a "win-win situation" (18) make sense to you? Why or why not?

- What problems or potential problems are associated with growing soybeans in the Amazon, and how do the benefits measure up to the costs?

Writing Activities

- Compare/contrast Blairo Maggi's approach to managing the rainforest to 19th- and 20th- century U.S. attitudes about our natural resources such as redwood forests, water, fish, or others. (See "The Redwoods Point the Way," "The Drying of the West," and "Still Waters: The Global Fish Crisis" in this collection.)

- After doing some research on the role U.S. businesses play in Brazil's soybean industry, write an essay that evaluates the extent to which they have acted responsibly with respect to environmental and social concerns. Based on what you find, rate their activities in these two areas.

- Write an essay that explains the problem of Amazonian deforestation and the conservation efforts that have been put in place so far. In your opinion, do the measures taken to protect the remaining rainforest meet the challenges at hand? Which threats to the forest appear to be the most serious, as you see them, and what hope, if any, can be found in the available solutions?

- Write an essay that examines the importance of the Amazonian rainforest as it relates to any of the following global issues: climate change, food and water shortages, displacement of indigenous people, poverty, or environmental and human exposure to contamination. (See "The End of Plenty," "The Big Melt," and "Water Pressure" in this collection.)

Collaborative Activities

- As a group, list the specific challenges to "social environmentalism" in the Amazon and the events that can be linked to the rise of this concept there. Make sure to define your terms.

- Discuss the ways the concept of the rainforest appears in advertising or other commercial contexts. In what ways has your image of the rainforest been influenced by advertising, by direct information, or by other sources of information? Have efforts to raise public awareness about the rainforest succeeded?

THE REDWOODS
POINT THE WAY

In his essay, J. Michael Fay's personal investigation of the status of the U.S. redwood forest tells a story of over a century of devastation "shaped by greed and waste." Asking us to question "the wisdom" of past approaches to forest management, he provides some compelling reasons to reconsider the redwoods as an important symbol of why conservation matters and what is at stake.

As you read "The Redwoods Point the Way," consider the following questions:

- How much old-growth redwood forest remains?
- Why, according to Fay, is the recovery of redwood forests important?
- What is Fay's purpose in connecting the policies of President Theodore Roosevelt at the beginning of the 20th century and those of President Obama at the onset of the 21st century?

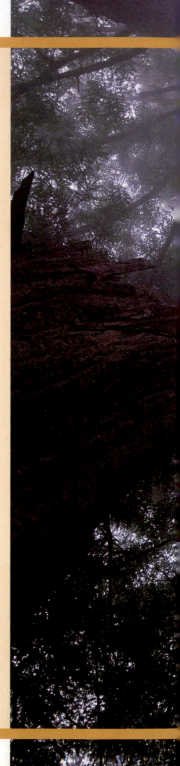

THE
REDWOODS
POINT
THE WAY

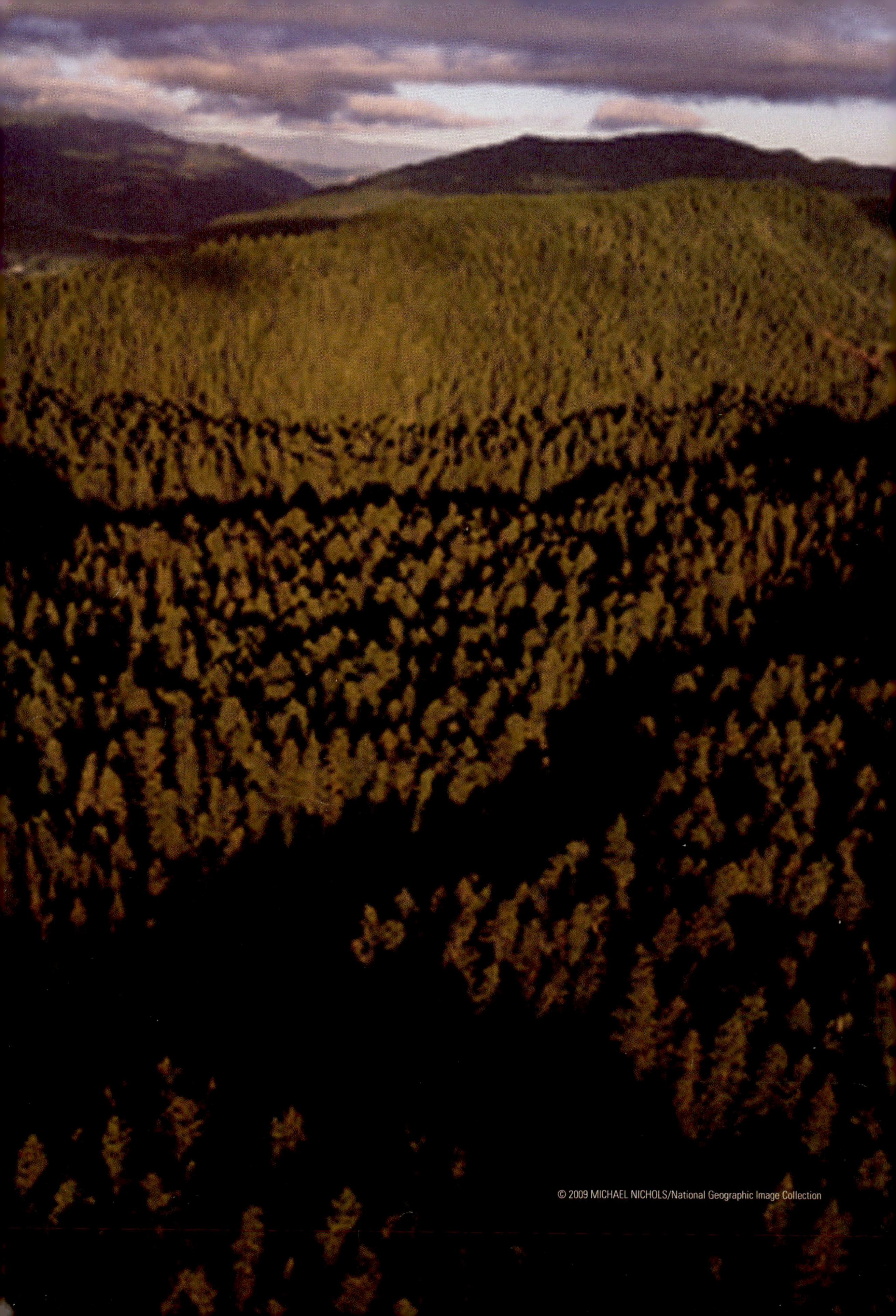

A NEW WAVE OF ENLIGHTENED FORESTRY

AS A MODEL FOR WISER STEWARDSHIP OF NATURE.

> They might think **I'm a gun-toting, right-wing redneck, but what they have to understand is, they've got our attention.**

On day 323 of the transect, in Jedediah Smith Redwoods State Park, I dropped over a log 18 feet in diameter into an abyss of giant botanical pickup sticks, deadfall that had piled up amid the living trees over thousands of years. Another fallen monster loomed. Grabbing huckleberry roots and clumps of sword ferns, I hauled myself and my 60-pound pack up its organic wall onto a trunk as long as a football field. Filthy and exhausted, surrounded by hundreds of towering redwood columns that were raining their captured fog on my head, I stood there overwhelmed by a scene straight out of the Jurassic.

I've been walking in forests for 40 years; never could I have imagined a woods as grand as this.

Staring skyward through the somber silhouettes, I thought about the timberman who had described his company's patchwork of clearcuts, with their sun-drenched mix of tiny trees interspersed with strips of older redwoods, as functionally the same as an old-growth forest. No amount of persuasive conversation or data will ever convince me of that. This isn't about loving big trees. It's about the fact that I spent 333 days walking 1,800 miles through the entire range of the redwoods with a notebook in my hand, documenting details about this ecosystem—and witnessing the aftermath of the cutting of at least 95 percent of the most wood-laden forest on Earth.

Timber folks know the history—most I met in redwood country used words like nuked, hammered, blitzed, wasted, and raped to describe the logging of the past. The landscape bears them out. I spent too many days on the transect pushing past gigantic stumps, through weedy stands of small trees amid crumbling road systems, over eroded hillsides, and across rivers choked with gravel and silt, whose fisheries had collapsed. It was a landscape shaped by greed and waste.

Adapted from "The Redwoods Point the Way" by J. Michael Fay: National Geographic Magazine, October 2009.

The time to argue about the wisdom of liquidating the resource base of the planet is over.

In the redwoods I found many who agree. Dave Lewers, whom I joined on the 12,000-acre Flat Ridge Ranch he meticulously manages in Sonoma County, said it best: "They might think I'm a gun-toting, right-wing redneck, but what they have to understand is, they've got our attention." The "they" are environmentalists and state regulators, and what Lewers meant was that he is a frontline participant in efforts to restore the redwood forest.

All along the transect I met foresters, owners, and loggers who talk as if they've discovered the holy grail of redwood management. People like Jim Able, Jim Greig, and Ed Tunheim who have found a way to bring vigor back to this ecosystem—and stay in business at the same time. What they're learning, and how they're applying that knowledge, can serve as a blueprint for the entire redwood range. Their ability to supply large amounts of lumber for humanity and improve ecosystem function is an approach that should be adopted around the world.

In brief: These veteran foresters are carrying out a form of single-tree selection that is more productive in the long term than clear-cutting. Every 10 to 15 years they take about a third of the timber in a stand, going for the least robust trees—the runts, as Jim Able calls them. This creates more open space, allowing the remaining trees to get a greater share of the sunlight, which speeds their growth. Every year the amount and quality of the standing wood increase, and because regeneration happens gradually, the process can proceed for centuries. The advantages are

> **The next quantum leap is is the idea that we can, and should, put a dollar value on the environmental assets of the forest.**

twofold: short-term income and a larger payback over the long term. "You can't be greedy or in a rush," Ed Tunheim says.

This isn't just about wood. Past damage to ecosystems is being repaired. Sediment is being excavated from streams to restore their original beds, and culverts enlarged to permit natural stream flow. Thousands of logs are being placed in creeks to create fish habitat. Roads are being recontoured and reinforced or simply erased from the landscape. Along rivers and in slide-prone areas, timber harvests are being reduced. Trees identified as crucial for wildlife habitat—and remnant old growth—are being preserved.

The next quantum leap is the idea that we can, and should, put a dollar value on the environmental assets of the forest. Already, some timber owners, helped by grants from voter-approved initiatives, are going above and beyond what state regulations require in rehabilitating watersheds, decommissioning roads, and stopping erosion. These investments reduce their maintenance costs and help the bottom line while guaranteeing benefits such as cleaner water and healthier fish populations.

Especially promising is the idea that because forests absorb the greenhouse gas carbon dioxide, timber owners should be paid for the carbon accumulated in their trees. The redwood forest, with its vast carbon-storage capacity, is where many of the first carbon sales have occurred. As new state and federal climate regulations take effect, this market will grow, along with the incentive for timber owners to maximize the standing volume and the productivity of their forests, which produce higher quality lumber the older they get.

© 2009 MICHAEL NICHOLS/National Geographic Image Collection

The time is right to embrace a systematic plan of recovery for the entire redwood forest—all the pieces are now in place.

The redwoods hold a broader lesson. In 1908 President Teddy Roosevelt brought together the governors of 39 states and territories, the Supreme Court justices, virtually his entire Cabinet, and members of Congress and 68 professional societies. Never before or since has such a powerful group been assembled in the White House. Opening the conference, Roosevelt said, "You have come hither at my request...to consider the question of the conservation and use of the great fundamental sources of wealth of this Nation. ... It is the chief material question that confronts us."

The President tallied the toll on the United States's resources, including the loss of half our original timber. He made an eloquent call to rebuild the nation's natural capital, or face hardship. He implored those in a position to exploit nature for excessive profit to take the moral high ground instead of robbing future generations.

At that time, a century ago, there were only about 300,000 white-tailed deer left in the entire United States. Today, even though the human footprint has increased exponentially, there are perhaps 30 million. This rehabilitation, in which states managed hunting, reintroduced the animals in hundreds of places, and restored habitat, has been so successful that many now consider whitetails a pest. The deer story Roosevelt helped inspire is a clear and simple demonstration that conservation can vastly increase the renewable resources we've hammered and wasted since Europeans arrived in North America.

Here is my message: President Obama, convene your own White House conference. The objective would be to build on what's being done in the redwoods and design a Marshall Plan for the proper use of all the natural assets in the United States. People will try to dissuade you, saying we can't possibly afford to think about saving nature when the world is mired in an economic crisis, confronting wars and the threat of nuclear terrorism. President Roosevelt, too, had his challenges—Japan and Russia at war, monopolists to control, the Panama Canal to build—but he understood that conservation was the principal material question facing humanity.

In the 21st century, as we face the consequences of global warming, this is even more vitally true. We need to generalize this simple notion: Rebuild our natural capital thoughtfully and reap the benefits. With increased production for humanity also come healthy ecosystems and global balance. We can—and must—do this not just with our forests and wildlife but also with the fish in our oceans and streams, the soils on our farms, and the grass in our pastures. The redwoods can show us the way.

Discussion Questions

- What techniques does the author use to capture and hold the reader's attention in this essay?

- What is Fay's purpose in linking the common interests of foresters, owners, and loggers?

- What does Fay mean by the "the environmental assets of the forests," and why is this concept important to his thesis?

- How does the author use contrast to highlight the importance of historical information and integrate it with the personal?

Writing Activities

- Write an essay that defines "national capital" and explains in detail how you understand its value on a national and global scale in the 21st century. Include effective examples to illustrate your points.

- Fay claims that "the time to argue about the wisdom of liquidating the resource base of the planet is over" (28). Apply his statement to examples from this and at least two other essays in this collection. In your view, is the author's urgency justified? Explain your position in detail, supporting it with relevant examples from the readings you have selected.

- Does the author's optimism about the actions taken so far to restore the redwood forest convince you that this ecosystem can be saved, considering the damage done over the past century or more? Write an essay in which you evaluate both the status of the forest and the measures Fay presents, and argue whether or not, in your view, a substantial recovery is possible. Provide well-chosen supporting details to illustrate your points.

- After doing a little research, compare/ contrast the role conservation played in the 20th century and the role it plays—or perhaps it should play—now. Consider our national priorities, global threats to the environment, population demands, or other large-scale issues that you think are important in relation to decisions about conservation, including the redwoods as a central theme in your essay.

Collaborative Activities

- As a group, make a list of parallels between the state of the environment and world issues in 1908 and at the present moment. Discuss how our relationship with the environment has changed or stayed the same over the past century.

- Working with a partner or two, discuss your previous knowledge related to redwoods and redwood forests. Combine your prior knowledge and experience. In what ways do Fay's observations and his viewpoint change or deepen your understanding of the ecological role redwoods play, their commercial value, and their value as a renewable resource?

WATER PRESSURE

Fen Montaigne's article presents a variety of approaches to solving what has become an increasingly serious global problem, and it offers some examples that dramatically illustrate how and why water distress impacts different regions.

As you read "Water Pressure," consider the following questions:

- Where can common ground be found in solving the world's water problems?
- What kinds of resources—and ideas—are needed to tackle increasing water shortages, as the world's demand continues to outpace the available sources of water on the planet?
- Where have the most promising approaches been developed?

Drawing deep from a new well, Soti Sotiar is among a lucky few: the 10 to 20 percent of rural Ethiopians with access to clean drinking water.

WATER PRESSURE

Photographs by Peter Essick

MEXICO CITY'S LEAKY SINK

Population booming as water pipes crumble, Mexico City must truck water to many residents. Once called the Venice of the New World for now long-gone lakes and canals, the city has so drained its aquifer since 1900 that it has sunk two dozen feet. As ground shifts, pipes break; leaks claim nearly a third of its water.

CHALLENGES FOR HUMANITY THE EARTH'S SIX BILLION PEOPLE ALREADY OVERTAX ITS SUPPLY OF ACCESSIBLE FRESH WATER.

WHAT HAPPENS WHEN THE PLANET GETS A FEW BILLION MORE HANDS?

Rajendra Singh came to the village, bringing with him the promise of water. If ever a place needed moisture, this hamlet in the desiccated Indian state of Rajasthan was it. Always a dry spot, Rajasthan had suffered several years of drought, leaving remote villages like Goratalai with barely enough water to quench the thirst of their inhabitants. Farm plots had shriveled, and men had fled to the cities seeking work, leaving those behind to subsist on roti, corn, and chili paste. Desperate villagers appealed to a local aristocratic family, who in turn contacted Singh, a man renowned across western India for his ability to use traditional methods of capturing monsoon rains to supply water year-round.

Singh arrived in Goratalai on a warm February morning. The sky was robin's egg blue, the same color it had been since August when, everyone recalled, the last rains had fallen. He was greeted by a group of about 50 people waiting in a dirt square under a banyan tree. The men wore loose-fitting

> **If ever a place needed moisture, this hamlet in the desiccated Indian State of Rajasthan was it.**

cotton pantaloons and turbans of orange, maroon, and white. They were rail-thin, their faces burnished by the sun and distinguished by great mustaches that swept across hollow cheeks. The women were covered from head to toe in vivid orange, gold, and pink clothing, a counterpoint to the parched dun terrain of rock and scrub.

Singh smiled and addressed the villagers.

"How many households do you have?"

"Eighty."

"It's been four years without much rain," interjected a woman. "And we don't have a proper dam to catch the water."

"Do you have any spots where a dam could go?" asked Singh, 43, who has a full head of black hair and a thick beard, both flecked with gray.

"Yes, two spots."

"Will the whole village be willing to work there?"

Adapted from "Water Pressure" by Fen Montaigne: National Geographic Magazine, September 2002.

"Yes," they replied in chorus. The villagers, nearly all of them illiterate, had submitted a petition to Singh asking for help, their names represented by violet thumbprints on a smudged piece of paper.

"I would like to help you," Singh told them, "but the work has to be done by you. You will have to provide one-third of the project through your labor, and the remaining two-thirds I will arrange."

The villagers clapped, the women broke into song, and the group hiked across the rock-studded hills to a ravine, the women's silver ankle bracelets jangling as they walked. After a few minutes Singh—dressed in a light-golden blouse that fell to his knees and white pants—directed villagers to place stones in a 75-yard line between two hills. "This is an ideal site," he announced. His organization, Tarun Bharat Sangh, would provide the engineering advice and materials. The villagers would supply the sweat equity. The 30-foot-high earthen dam and reservoir, known as a *johad*, could be finished in three months, before the start of the monsoon. If the rains were plentiful, the reservoir would not only provide surface water for drinking and irrigation but would also recharge dry wells as water seeped into the ground.

"You shouldn't get disheartened," Singh told the villagers. "You will not see the results immediately. But soon the dam will begin to raise the water level in your wells."

Ninety minutes after he arrived, Singh was gone, heading to a nearby village that had also requested help building a johad. In recent years Singh's johads have sprung up all over Rajasthan—an estimated 4,500 dams in about 1,000 villages, all built using local labor and native materials. His movement has caught on, he told me, because it puts control over water in the hands of villagers. "*If they* feel a johad is their own, they will maintain it," said Singh.

Further deepening concern over what a World Bank expert calls the "grim arithmetic of water."

"This is a very sustainable, self-reliant system. I can say confidently that if we can manage rain in India in traditional ways, there will be sufficient water for our growing population."

Among the environmental specters confronting humanity in the 21st century—global warming, the destruction of rain forests, overfishing of the oceans—a shortage of fresh water is at the top of the list, particularly in the developing world. Hardly a month passes without a new study making another alarming prediction, further deepening concern over what a World Bank expert calls the "grim arithmetic of water." Recently the United Nations said that 2.7 billion people would face severe water shortages by 2025 if consumption continues at current rates. Fears about a parched future arise from a projected growth of world population from more than six billion today to an estimated nine billion in 2050. Yet the amount of fresh water on Earth is not increasing. Nearly 97 percent of the planet's water is salt water in seas and oceans. Close to 2 percent of Earth's water is frozen in polar ice sheets and glaciers, and a fraction of one percent is available for drinking, irrigation, and industrial use.

Gloomy water news, however, is not just a thing of the future: Today an estimated 1.2 billion people drink unclean water, and about 2.5 billion lack proper toilets or sewerage systems. More than five million people die each year from water-related diseases such as cholera and dysentery. All over the globe farmers and municipalities are pumping water out of the ground faster than it can be replenished.

Still, as I discovered on a two-month trip to Africa, India, and Spain, a host of individuals,

Last year in Matamoros, Mexico, the overused Rio Grande dropped below the city's water intake pipes, but that problem was temporary. With little wastewater treatment, the city's canals fester with sewage and industrial pollution.

organizations, and businesses are working to solve water's dismal arithmetic. Some are reviving ancient techniques such as rainwater harvesting, and others are using 21st-century technology. But all have two things in common: a desire to obtain maximum efficiency from every drop of water and a belief in using local solutions and free market incentives in their conservation campaigns.

That the planet's fresh water is consumed profligately is beyond doubt, particularly in agriculture, which accounts for 70 percent of all water use. Getting more out of each drop of water is imperative, for as the world's population increases and the demand for food soars, unchecked irrigation poses a serious threat to rivers, wetlands, and lakes. China's Yellow River, siphoned off by farmers and cities, has failed to reach the sea most years during the past decade. In North America not only does the Colorado River barely make it to the Gulf of California, but last year even the Rio Grande dried up before it merged with the Gulf of Mexico. In Central Asia the Aral Sea shrank by half after the Soviets began diverting water for cotton and other crops. Elsewhere, countless small rivers have gone dry.

To see what unbridled water consumption has wrought, both good and bad, you need go no farther than the Indian state of Gujarat. Like neighboring Rajasthan, Gujarat is a dry place that has experienced a surge of irrigated agriculture. In the northern part of the state, on a hot spring day, I came across a brick pump house amid flat green fields of wheat, mustard, cumin, and anise. Inside was the electrical system for a 62-horsepower motor that, ten hours a day, pumped a steady column of water from deep underground into a concrete tank through which the water was channeled to nearby fields. One of the pump's owners—70-year-old Nemchandbhai U. Patel—rested on a rope bed in the cool, dusky interior, lulled by the sound of water rushing up from underground aquifers and gurgling into the tank.

Patel stirred as I approached. He explained that the pump was used to irrigate his fields, as well as those of his partners and 50 other farmers who purchase the water. Without it they would have to rely solely on rain, which in an area that receives about 25 inches of precipitation a year—most of it in short summer cloudbursts—is a highly risky proposition. "Thanks to this well," said Patel, "we are able to sustain our lives."

The electric pump that sent water streaming onto Patel's land is the machine that has powered India's green revolution. That agricultural achievement, which has enabled the country to grow enough food for its one billion people, was accomplished because of a huge increase in groundwater pumping. In the mid-fifties fewer than 100,000 motorized pumps were extracting groundwater for Indian agriculture. Today about 20 million are in operation, with the number growing by half a million each year.

But the unregulated use of so much groundwater has come at a high price: With farmers extracting water more quickly than nature can replenish it, aquifers have been depleted to the point that roughly half of India now faces overpumping problems, such as groundwater shortages or the influx of salt water into coastal wells. Many farmers have been forced to abandon wells or keep drilling deeper, raising costs and driving some out of business. In parts of Gujarat the water table has been dropping as much as 20 feet a year. Four decades ago the water table under Nemchandbhai Patel's fields was at 100 feet; now he must drill 500 feet before he hits water. He keeps deepening

We think this water may one day be lost to us forever.

his well, but to drill a new one could be prohibitively expensive.

"We think this water may one day be lost to us forever," said Mohanbhai G. Patel, 67, a nearby well owner whose last name is shared by many in the region. "The water we are now pumping from deep underground has been accumulating for thousands of years. It's like this urn here. If you keep drinking water and never refill it, at some point there will be no more. Unless the government brings in major schemes to recharge these aquifers, we will not survive."

One reason farmers in India, and throughout the world, have been heedlessly pumping water is that they have paid so little for it In India the water itself is free, and the government heavily subsidizes the electricity that drives the pumps. Rather than pay for the number of hours a pump runs, farmers pay a low, flat annual rate and pump with abandon.

The overpumping of aquifers, whether for agricultural or municipal use, extends far beyond India. U.S. farmers are withdrawing water from the Ogallala aquifer, which underlies the Great Plains, at an unsustainable rate, with a third of the Texas portion already significantly depleted. The water table under the North China Plain, which produces about half of China's wheat and corn, is steadily dropping. Sandra Postel, a freshwater expert and director of the Massachusetts-based Global Water Policy Project, said that continuing groundwater depletion could reduce China's and India's grain production by 10 to 20 percent in the coming decades.

Two decades ago, as an idealistic young man intent on helping India's rural poor, Rajendra Singh traveled to northwestern Rajasthan, which was suffering water shortages from excessive groundwater extraction. Shortly after he arrived in the impoverished Alwar district, two things became clear to Singh. The first was that managing water wisely was the key to helping drought-prone villages in the region. The second was that farmers were pumping far too much groundwater.

"If you replenish water, that is a green revolution," Singh told me. "But if you destroy your water capital, what kind of green revolution is that?"

An old villager showed Singh the numerous earthen dams in the district that had fallen into disrepair, their reservoirs filled with silt. They were remnants of a rainwater collection tradition that dated back 5,000 years in India, a system that used the natural terrain to channel and store the brief monsoon downpours for year-round use. But community rainwater collection schemes fell out of favor during British rule and after independence in 1947; their neglect, coupled with overpumping of groundwater, led to a crisis in villages throughout western India. Singh became consumed with the idea of building johads, gradually helping villagers erect the earthen and stone structures all over Rajasthan.

Today he is perhaps the best known of a large group of people who have revived India's ancient rainwater harvesting techniques, which use not only dams but also underground storage tanks and large concrete-lined reservoirs. Singh's organization—financed by the Ford Foundation, among others—has 45 full-time employees and 230 part-time workers. He spends eight months a year on the road, rarely seeing his wife and son and often sleeping in the backseat of his chauffeur-driven car at night, no small hardship given India's chaotic, treacherous, and polluted highways.

I joined Singh for two days, traveling to a handful of villages where johads had spurred an economic revival. The success of his movement owes much to his personality, which has inspired villagers to follow his lead during the arduous process of building dams, often with

their bare hands. His manner is gentle and unflappable, and he spends hours listening to villagers, sometimes sleeping in their huts and eating their food. In the hamlet of Johdi Ki Dhani, where Singh initiated the construction of three johads, the headman said Singh's quiet, persistent ways overcame the residents' initial skepticism.

"Rajendra Singh used to come as a very simple person," said Suraj Mal Gujur, 45. "He would sit among us and not act like a big shot. He eventually established a very close relationship with us."

One of the villages Singh and I visited was Neemi, situated in dry hills about 20 miles from Rajasthan's capital, Jaipur. Neemi's farmers had pumped many of their wells dry, and some were abandoning the land for work in nearby cities. Singh helped them build several large dams, and by the end of the 1990s the reservoirs began recharging depleted groundwater, catalyzing what villagers describe as a remarkable turnaround in Neemi's fortunes.

Today Neemi is a thriving village in a fertile valley, its fields green with wheat, vegetables, watermelons, and flowers. Not only has migration to the cities stopped, but more than 400 farmworkers have also poured into Neemi to cultivate its fruit and vegetables. With more water and fodder available, the number of cattle among Neemi's 122 dairy farmers has increased sharply, quadrupling the village's milk production.

Singh attributes the growing success of his movement to a basic fact: It encourages local people to build smaller dams and reservoirs in their own backyards, rather than relying on large government-built dams, which often displace residents and transfer water far away.

"This work fulfills the need of the self-reliance of local people," said Singh. "In a small project everyone can participate in decision-making. That's the only real way to improve a community. The community gets employment and has a feeling of ownership and control."

Sunita Narain, director of the nonprofit Center for Science and Environment in New Delhi, said rainwater harvesting is not a panacea and needs to be coupled with conservation measures and, on occasion, the big public works projects Singh abhors. Still, the work of Singh and others has had a profound impact in India, she said, and is proof of an axiom in the developing world: "Managing water well," said Narain, "is the first step in alleviating poverty."

The Katuba region, north of the Zambian capital of Lusaka, is not chronically short of water. But it is awash in poverty, and the trick—as Paul Polak knows well—is getting the water from where it lies to farmers' fields, a straightforward task that can bring cash trickling into rural villages.

Polak, a 68-year-old Coloradan fond of wearing orange tennis shoes and suspenders, has spent much of his adult life figuring out how to get water cheaply from point A to point B in the developing world. His own path has not been quite so direct. He was a psychiatrist, who in his extensive travels grew increasingly interested in reducing poverty. Gradually it became clear to Polak that to improve the lives of hundreds of millions of subsistence farmers, water was the starting point.

"You could see how essential water was to alleviating poverty," said Polak. "If you wanted to do anything, you had to start with these small farmers and irrigation. The power to control water is absolutely crucial to them. That fact should shape all development policy."

Polak's shrewd investments in oil and real estate allowed him to spend more time working on improving water delivery to the poor. In 1981 he formed the nonprofit International Development Enterprises (IDE), which has played a major role in disseminating treadle

This work fulfills the need of the self-reliance of local people.

pumps in several countries, such as Bangladesh, which has 1.3 million. This StairMaster-like device enables farmers to transfer shallow groundwater to their fields by stepping up and down on pedals that drive the pump.

Like Rajendra Singh, Polak is convinced that farmers must have a stake in the technology that brings them water. Polak is now the full-time head of IDE, which has a staff of 542 working in seven countries. The organization sells treadle pumps through its own network of local distributors, usually for less than a hundred dollars. Polak's ultimate goal, indicative of his penchant to think big, is to bring treadle pumps or low-cost drip irrigation to 30 million farm families in the developing world.

His efforts in sub-Saharan Africa recently brought him to Zambia. I joined him there as he investigated the irrigation potential of seasonal wetlands called *dambos*, from which water can be easily extracted by a treadle pump. Polak and his staff had estimated that 500,000 farmers living near dambos and other shallow water sources in sub-Saharan Africa could use treadle pumps for irrigation, and what he saw in Zambia did not disabuse him of that notion. Traveling from Lusaka to Victoria Falls in the south, Polak met dozens of farmers using buckets to water their fields. It is a backbreaking, inefficient way to irrigate, and the farmers told Polak they would welcome a treadle pump to reduce the drudgery and increase production.

Evidence of what a treadle pump can do in Africa was on display in the countryside around Katuba, an area of rolling savanna and open woodlands. Most villagers there earn less than a dollar a day, and they live in clusters of grass-roofed mud huts, around which they cultivate small plots of corn, Zambia's staple food. The surrounding hills are dotted with acacias and graceful mopani trees.

Late in the day, with thick white clouds sailing across the sky, Polak stopped at several huts owned by two brothers, Noah and Shadreck Phiri. Short, tautly muscled men in their 30s, the Phiris were among 2,000 Zambians who have bought IDE treadle pumps over the past five years. Polak greeted the brothers warmly and pulled out a clipboard. With his gray hair and gentle demeanor, he cut a grandfatherly figure, but, as I quickly learned, he is a senior citizen with a workaholic edge. He skipped lunch as he led his entourage around for hours under the scorching midday sun; at night, as he was driven to the next town, Polak would fall asleep in mid-sentence, nodding off during a discourse on Zambian agricultural markets.

Now he launched into a 15-minute interrogation, and it soon emerged that the Phiris had been struggling in their pre-pump days, relying solely on bucket irrigation. The pump, which they bought two years ago, enabled them to expand their fields to about 1.5 acres and grow valuable cash crops, such as baby corn, green beans, and paprika peppers. Their annual income had tripled to $400 apiece. Now they can feed their children more meat, pay their school fees, and replace the earthen floors of their huts with concrete. The brothers told Polak they had visions of cultivating more land, hiring laborers, and paying to bring electricity to their homes. "I want to build a very nice house, and put sheet metal on the roof instead of grass," said Shadreck.

The treadle pump, which had a blue metal frame and two-by-fours as pedals, was sitting in the doorway of Noah's hut. It was summer—the rainy season in southern Africa—but rain had been scarce, and Noah was irrigating his fields several times a week. Two of his daughters picked up the pump and carried it to the dambo, which was 150 yards wide and thick with reeds and banana plants. They hooked one end to a pipe that extended from a shallow, open well at the edge of the dambo and connected the other end to a 50-yard piece of black plastic pipe that ran to a field of Chinese cabbage. Noah placed his bare, callused feet on the two-by-fours and began high-stepping in a steady rhythm that he can maintain for the several hours needed to irrigate his fields. Water began gushing onto the light brown earth, splashing the cabbage leaves.

Polak cites estimates that sub-Saharan Africa contains 20 million acres of dambos. Scientists are just beginning to study the impact of irrigation on these wetlands, but he believes that treadle pumps, which withdraw far less water than motorized pumps, do not seriously damage dambos. The potential benefits, he said, are immense.

If the Phiri brothers are at one end of the spectrum of the world's irrigators, then Kallie Schoeman must surely be somewhere near the other. A sixth-generation Afrikaner, Schoeman presides over South Africa's largest family-owned citrus farm, an operation that covers 4,400 acres in the fertile, heavily irrigated Olifants River Valley. The Schoeman farm has 500,000 citrus trees that annually produce 175 million oranges and lemons for export to 32 countries. At the heart of this flourishing enterprise is a sophisticated irrigation system that points the way to the changes farmers must make as water becomes scarcer and more expensive.

Since joining the family business 27 years ago, Schoeman has helped introduce a succession of irrigation technologies. When he began, the farm simply opened the sluice gates of irrigation canals and flooded the citrus groves, a highly inefficient system still common in the world today. In the 1980s more efficient sprinklers were introduced. Now Schoeman is steadily replacing the sprinklers with super-efficient drip irrigation, which "gives the trees exactly what they need every day," he said, by parceling out small amounts of water to each tree. As Schoeman has used ever more efficient irrigation systems, the farm has quadrupled the production of fruit per acre while actually using a third of the water.

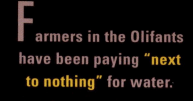
Farmers in the Olifants have been paying "next to nothing" for water.

The nerve endings of his present system are yard-long computerized probes that the irrigation manager, Jaco Burger, places in the soil beneath tidy rows of trees. Every 15 minutes, via solar-powered radio, the probes relay data about soil moisture to the farm's computers. Based on that information and the time of year—the trees need different amounts of water during the different stages of fruit development—Burger adjusts the rate at which water, mixed with fertilizer, flows. Standing in a hundred-acre field, surrounded by about 35,000 young orange trees, I watched as water trickled from a narrow tube into the soil below a sapling—one of three 20-minute feeding pulses the trees would receive that day.

Burger said commercial farmers will have to continue making such technological leaps as water becomes costlier. As he put it, farmers in the Olifants have been paying "next to nothing" for water. But that, and many other aspects of water in South Africa, are beginning to change. In 1998 the government passed the National Water Act, which is designed, in part, to redress the legacy of apartheid by assuring that everyone has equal access to water. The law looks at river basins as ecological systems, requiring that basic human needs, such as clean drinking water, and basic environmental needs, such as maintaining stream flows, be met before giving water to industry and agriculture.

"We know agriculture won't get more water," said Schoeman. "We will get less, it will become more expensive, and we will have to use it more efficiently."

Another South African with an obsessive desire to make the most of every drop of water is Neil Macleod, the man in charge of providing water and sewerage services to roughly three million people in Durban. A plain-spoken, unassuming civil engineer of 50 with a brush mustache, Macleod has drastically reduced waste in the city's water system while simultaneously improving water delivery to the urban poor.

Taking over as executive director of Durban Metro Water Services in 1992, two years before the end of apartheid, Macleod encountered an abysmal situation. Durban had one million people living in the city proper and another 1.5 million people, almost all black, who had moved into shantytowns or were living in housing projects just outside the city. Macleod and his engineers determined that 42 percent of the region's water was being wasted because of broken water pipes and mains, leaky toilets, and faulty plumbing. Of particular concern were two large districts, with a combined population of 500,000, where up to 87 percent of the water was being lost due to leaks and other wastage.

"People were not paying for water, and if a shower or toilet was broken, it just ran," recalled Macleod. "We inherited 700 reported leaks and bursts. The water literally just ran down the streets. Demand for water was growing 4 percent a year, and we thought we'd have to build another dam by 2000."

Macleod embarked on a crash program to tame the colossal losses. His crews began repairing and replacing mains. They put meters on residences, replaced four-gallon flush toilets with two-gallon models, and retrofitted wasteful showerheads and water taps. To ensure that the poor would receive a basic supply of water, Macleod installed tanks in homes and apartments to provide 50 gallons of water a day free to each household.

Water consumption in metropolitan Durban is now less than it was in 1996, even as 800,000 more people have received service.

By cutting water use—daily consumption in the most wasteful districts has been reduced by more than half—Durban's conservation measures paid for themselves within a year. Plans to build a costly new dam have been shelved, and Macleod is confident that no new dams will be needed in the coming decades, despite the expected addition of about 300,000 users.

Around the world other water conservation programs have also achieved impressive results. U.S. cities such as Boston, Seattle, and Albuquerque have reduced demand 20 to 25 percent in part by repairing aging infrastructure and retrofitting plumbing fixtures in homes. Indeed, per capita indoor water use in the United States has dropped since 1980. Outdoor use, however, has risen, probably because so many people have installed automatic lawn sprinkler systems. Today, the average American uses 101 gallons of water a day—more than 15 times that used by many people in developing countries.

In Durban, Macleod has now turned to water recycling. With the region's water supplier increasing prices, he decided to take about 10 million of the 125 million gallons of wastewater the city treated daily and use it again, piping it to industries nearby. The French firm Vivendi, one of a growing number of companies involved in water management, built a sophisticated treatment facility next to one of Durban's wastewater plants. Operators of a nearby paper mill and refinery are satisfied because they pay almost half price for the recycled water, and Macleod is pleased because the recycling has cut metropolitan water demand by about 5 percent.

On a steamy afternoon Macleod took me to the plant, where I watched wastewater turned into clean water in just 12 hours as it passed through sand and carbon filters, was treated with ozone, and dosed with chlorine. I finished the tour on the roof of the Vivendi facility, where glasses of water were arrayed on a table. I took several sips and could not discern a difference between the municipal drinking water and the treated wastewater. Though intended for industrial use, the recycled water I sampled was pure enough for drinking.

The sweet taste of the treated wastewater was a taste of the future, for in the years to come water recycling will likely become increasingly common. Indeed, in the neighboring desert nation of Namibia, Vivendi is a partner in a plant that turns wastewater directly into drinking water for the capital, Windhoek, refining the water even one step further than Durban's recycling operation. Windhoek's wastewater-to-drinking water plant is the only such facility in the world, but Stephen McCarley, the general manager of Vivendi's Durban operation, is confident it won't be the last.

"As water goes up in price, the opportunities to do this kind of treatment will grow," said McCarley, my guide on the tour of the Durban plant. "From the technological point of view, you can do anything with water. As the resource is more constrained, people will have to get used to recycling."

Noting the purity of the treated wastewater, Macleod chimed in, "Go to many areas of the world, and they're drinking far worse water than this."

Macleod would not have to go far. His own province of KwaZulu-Natal was fighting a cholera outbreak, proof that post-apartheid South Africa—despite its water pioneers and progressive water legislation—still has a huge gap between blacks and whites. The South African government has succeeded in bringing safe drinking water to millions of its citizens in recent years, but about 7 million of the country's 44 million people still lack access to clean water within 200 yards of their homes. Drinking contaminated water, often from streams, was behind the most recent outbreak, which has killed 289 people in

KwaZulu-Natal and infected 120,000 others since August 2000. Those deaths were among the 18,000 that occur in South Africa annually from diarrhea-related ailments, most of which are waterborne.

The outbreak was centered in the hilly, picturesque Ladysmith region, where whites typically have water and sewerage systems, but where 85 percent of blacks lack proper sanitation and 60 percent do not have access to the South African government's minimum recommended quantity of clean water: 25 liters (6.6 gallons) per person per day.

I visited rural health clinics where patients lay under canvas tents, receiving rehydration fluid, intravenously and orally, to counteract the cholera infection, which can cause rapid death from diarrhea-induced dehydration.

In the Mhlumayo area, along a feeble stream called Impundu, I met the family of one of the victims, a 59-year-old farmer named Mkhanyis-wa Sithole. I found his wife and several of their eight children amid a cluster of huts perched on a hillside. Khithiza Sithole, 53, was a regal woman in a long, blue mourning dress. She sat on a grass mat and recounted how her husband fell ill around 4 a.m. on November 26, 2001.

"The diarrhea started, and he was crying about the pain in his stomach," said Mrs. Sithole. "He was vomiting and having bad cramps. He kept crying out."

Shortly after noon the family drove him to a rural clinic, where he was given intravenous fluids. His condition worsened, however, and he was transferred by ambulance to Ladysmith Hospital. There, despite continued treatment, he died around 11 p.m., less than 24 hours after falling ill. The family suspects that he may have contracted cholera after drinking directly from the Impundu. Several other people in the village also died.

I n western europe and the United States people have long since lost their fear of dying from a drink of water. Nevertheless, water use there poses an altogether different threat, this one to nature itself.

In the Castile La Mancha region of south-central Spain, a 74-year-old former fisherman, Julio Escudero, has seen one of the country's prized wetlands altered beyond recognition. Escudero was born on the banks of Las Tablas de Daimiel, a freshwater marsh at the heart of a sprawling, 60,000-acre mosaic of wetlands in La Mancha. He was part of a small fishing community of 300 families around Daimiel that harvested primarily carp and crayfish. Escudero sometimes fished on the picturesque Guadiana River and fondly recalls an area called Los Ojos—"the eyes"—where large, underground springs bubbled up into the limpid waterway.

"We could see all the water rising from the bottom in big columns," said Escudero. "I would sit in my boat six or seven meters away and just watch the water coming up. Now it looks like the moon."

Los Ojos is no more: The underwater springs dried up in 1984. That stretch of the Guadiana—a six-mile portion above Daimiel—also has disappeared. Where there was once a gentle, percolating river, 30 yards wide, there now are a road, fields of grain, and rocky portions of riverbed. The 60,000 acres of original wetlands, superb habitat for cranes and waterfowl, have shrunk to a core area of about 14,000 acres.

What happened? An onslaught of irrigated agriculture. La Mancha has witnessed an explosion of well digging in the past 40 years that has lowered the water table and reduced streamflows. The number of irrigated acres—farmers grow alfalfa, barley, corn, wheat, and sugar beets, among other crops—has soared from 60,000 in 1960 to 500,000 today, and the number of wells has grown from 1,500 to an official count of 21,000. Some experts say the total number, including illegal wells, could surpass 50,000.

"As long as you have so many wells sucking out the groundwater, Las Tablas won't come back," said Escudero, the last commercial fisherman to work in Las Tablas de Daimiel. "I see no solution. I see a cadaver."

Spain is now at a crossroads. Like another semiarid region, southern California, this Mediterranean country has built dams—about 1,200 major ones—and piped water long distances to supply farms and municipalities. Now a new National Hydrological Plan calls for transferring nearly 1.4 billion cubic yards of water a year from the Ebro River in the north to burgeoning regions along the Mediterranean coast. The plan has stirred controversy, with a growing number of opponents questioning the cost, economic and environmental, of such massive schemes. The government says the multibillion-dollar project is necessary to halt the overexploitation of southern aquifers. But environmentalists contend that the Ebro has already lost half its flow because of irrigation and dams and will shrink even further, accelerating the decline of the Ebro Delta, a prime Mediterranean fish nursery and vital bird habitat.

Spanish environmentalists say it is time to stop draining the country's wetlands and to curtail agricultural subsidies that underwrite the cultivation of irrigated crops, encouraging profligate water use. Spain's greatest wetland—Doñana on the Atlantic coast, home to half a million overwintering birds and a stopover for six million migratory birds—has seen its natural marshlands cut from about 370,000 acres to 75,000 because of agricultural development and water engineering projects. (Despite such losses, Doñana still attracts large numbers of flamingos, white storks, glossy ibises, greylag geese, and other waterfowl because the wetlands were converted to flooded rice fields or aquaculture ponds.) The government and conservation groups have now embarked on a major reengineering program—similar to an eight-billion-dollar plan to restore water flows in the Florida Everglades—that will revive some of Doñana's marshes.

There is a kind of **silver bullet belief** about desalinization, but the fact is, water conservation is where the big gains are to be made.

This century many countries will face the dilemma being confronted by the people of Spain: how to balance human needs with the requirements of natural systems that are vital to sustain life on Earth. Some are hoping that new technologies, such as the desalination of seawater, will solve the problems faced by a water-stressed world. Yet only two-tenths of one percent of the water people use today is desalinated, and most of that is produced in desert kingdoms and island nations. Desalination is sure to become more common—plants are now under construction in southern California and Florida—but some experts remain skeptical that the process will become widespread, because of its cost.

"There is a kind of a silver bullet belief about desalination," said Sandra Postel of the Global Water Policy Project. "But the fact is, water conservation is where the big gains are to be made."

Indeed, during my travels I came away most impressed with the ingenuity of people like Rajendra Singh and Neil Macleod. The choice of heeding or ignoring such innovators is a stark one, as I saw in western India. In Gujarat's largest city, Ahmadabad, the Sabarmati River once flowed perennially through the heart of town. Today, due to the construction of a large dam and overpumping of

WATER BLUES OR A BLUE REVOLUTION?
Water is momentarily plentiful for a boy in the gush of a Calcutta well,
but as he grows into a man, India's water situation will likely go from bad
to worse. Another two billion people will need food and water by 2025.
Will the planet have enough water? That depends on how wisely it's used.

the region's aquifers, the river only runs during the monsoon floods in summer. The rest of the time the Sabarmati is what I saw last February—a dry, dust-shrouded scar inhabited by tens of thousands of people living in fetid squatters' shacks.

A few hundred miles to the north, in Rajasthan's Sariska Tiger Reserve, is another vision. There, in an arid mountain valley where residents once walked two miles to fetch water, Rajendra Singh has helped villagers construct several low dams. Where once there was a dry creek bed, now there are reservoirs. Lined by palms and looking very much like an oasis, their waters offer people what they have lacked for decades—a cool drink, close at hand.

Discussion Questions

- In what ways do the individual needs of different regions require unique solutions to water shortages?
- What role do innovative people play in reducing water distress around the world, compared to the role larger organizations might play?
- To what extent can education provide alternatives to profligate water use?
- How important is governmental intervention in changing water use among individuals, communities, and beyond?

Writing Activities

- Write an essay that evaluates the success of one innovative approach to water stress presented in this article. Explain whether or not this approach can be applied successfully in other regions or situations. If it can, offer some suggestions about how and where it might be successfully applied. If it can't, explain why not, and offer some suggestions about what is needed to bring different approaches to other areas.
- Do the creative approaches presented in this article inspire hope for larger and more widespread solutions? Write a position paper that argues whether or not we should be hopeful, supporting your viewpoint with clear evidence and well-chosen examples from the article and from your experience.
- Do you see government and conservation groups as allies or adversaries in solving water shortages at the community level and/or the national level? Write an essay that analyzes the roles as you see them and offers some suggestions about what

is required for them to work effectively toward solutions.

- Write an essay that argues for or against aggressive water restrictions in your community. Examine the needs and the challenges carefully. What obstacles might arise if such measures were taken, and how might these be addressed in a realistic program to conserve water in your area?

Collaborative Activities

- Working with one or two partners, examine the dilemma stated on page 45: "How to balance human needs the requirements of natural systems that are vital to sustain life on earth." Discuss possible reasons for giving preference to one or the other. Based on your discussion of the needs of both humans and the systems that support life on earth, write a paragraph together, explaining each side of the problem and offering some well reasoned suggestions as to how we might address this dilemma in the next decade.
- Form small groups whose members live near each other. Discuss the relevance of global water shortages to your region and/or the specific community in which you live. In what ways do your community's needs relate, or not, to global water shortages. Write a letter to your local newspaper that brings attention to the global water problems that may not otherwise be apparent to the typical American. Explain what members of your community should know about the world's water problems and what they can do, as a community, to improve conservation.

THE DRYING OF THE WEST

Robert Kunzig's article presents a new way of understanding the challenges that lie ahead in preserving the American West's future water supply. Evidence from ancient trees, as well as the disappearance of human communities over 500 years ago, suggests that we are witnessing a trend that portends megadroughts that may put the entire region in jeopardy and challenge the assumptions behind our use of water resources in the 20th century.

As You Read "The Drying of the West" consider the following questions:

- What views have influenced water use and development patterns in the Western states over the past century?

- What role have the study of tree rings and insect infestations played in our understanding of what lies in store in terms of climate change?

- How have assumptions about climate and natural resources guided our development of the Southwest, and in what ways have these assumptions put us at risk?

In drought-parched Los Padres National Forest in southern California, a helitanker douses a hot spot in the huge Zaca fire that erupted in July 2007, scorching 240,000 acres. Years of sparse rain primed the region for the second largest fire in California history.

THE DRYING OF THE WEST

Photographs by Vincent Laforet

THE AMERICAN WEST
WAS WON BY WATER MANAGEMENT.
WHAT HAPPENS WHEN THERE'S NO WATER LEFT TO MANAGE?

> **You really need a catastrophe to get people's attention.**

When provided with continuous nourishment, trees, like people, grow complacent.

Tree-ring scientists use the word to describe trees like those on the floor of the Colorado River Valley, whose roots tap into thick reservoirs of moist soil. Complacent trees aren't much use for learning about climate history, because they pack on wide new rings of wood even in dry years. To find trees that feel the same climatic pulses as the river, trees whose rings widen and narrow from year to year with the river itself, scientists have to climb up the steep, rocky slopes above the valley and look for gnarled, ugly trees, the kind that loggers ignore. For some reason such "sensitive" trees seem to live longer than the complacent ones. "Maybe you can get too much of a good thing," says Dave Meko.

Meko, a scientist at the Laboratory of Tree-Ring Research at the University of Arizona, has been studying the climate history of the western United States for decades. Tree-ring fieldwork is hardly expensive—you need a device called an increment borer to drill into the trees, you need plastic straws (available in a pinch from McDonald's) to store the pencil-thin cores you've extracted from bark to pith, and you need gas, food, and lodging. But during the relatively wet 1980s and early '90s, Meko found it difficult to raise even the modest funds needed for his work. "You don't generate interest to study drought unless you're in a drought," he says. "You really need a catastrophe to get people's attention," adds colleague Connie Woodhouse.

Then, in 2002, the third dry year in a row and the driest on record in many parts of the Southwest, the flow in the Colorado fell to a quarter of its long-term average. That got people's attention.

The Colorado supplies 30 million people in seven states and Mexico with water. Denver, Las Vegas, Phoenix, Tucson, Los Angeles, and San Diego all depend on it, and starting this year so will Albuquerque. It irrigates four million acres of farmland, much of which would otherwise be desert, but which now produces billions of dollars' worth of crops. Gauges first installed in the 19th century provide a measure of the flow of the river in acre-feet, one acre-foot being a foot of water spread over an acre, or about 326,000 gallons. Today the operation of the pharaonic

Adapted from "Drying of the West" by Robert Kunzig: National Geographic Magazine, February 2008.

infrastructure that taps the Colorado—the dams and reservoirs and pipelines and aqueducts—is based entirely on data from those gauges. In 2002 water managers all along the river began to wonder whether that century of data gave them a full appreciation of the river's eccentricities. With the lawns dying in Denver, a water manager there asked Woodhouse: How often has it been this dry?

Over the next few years Woodhouse, Meko, and some colleagues hunted down and cored the oldest drought-sensitive trees they could find growing in the upper Colorado basin, both living and dead. Wood takes a long time to rot in a dry climate; in Harmon Canyon in eastern Utah, Meko found one Douglas fir log that had laid down its first ring as a sapling in 323 B.C. That was an extreme case, but the scientists still collected enough old wood to push their estimates of annual variations in the flow of the Colorado back deep into the Middle Ages. The results came out last spring. They showed that the Colorado has not always been as generous as it was throughout the 20th century.

The California Department of Water Resources, which had funded some of the research, published the results as an illustrated poster. Beneath a series of stock southwestern postcard shots, the spiky trace of tree-ring data oscillates nervously across the page, from A.D. 762 on the left to 2005 on the right. One photo shows the Hoover Dam, water gushing from its outlets. When the dam was being planned in the 1920s to deliver river water to the farms of the Imperial Valley and the nascent sprawl of Los Angeles, the West, according to the tree rings, was in one of the wettest quarter centuries of the past millennium. Another photo shows the booming skyline of San Diego, which doubled its population between 1970 and 2000—again, an exceptionally wet period along the river. But toward the far left of the poster, there is a picture of Spruce Tree House, one of the spectacular

The wet 20th century, the wettest of the past millennium, the century when Americans built an incredible civilization in the desert, is over.

cliff dwellings at Mesa Verde National Park in southwestern Colorado, a pueblo site abandoned by the Anasazi at the end of the 13th century. Underneath the photo, the graph reveals that the Anasazi disappeared in a time of exceptional drought and low flow in the river.

In fact, the tree rings testified that in the centuries before Europeans settled the Southwest, the Colorado basin repeatedly experienced droughts more severe and protracted than any since then. During one 13-year megadrought in the 12th century, the flow in the river averaged around 12 million acre-feet, 80 percent of the average flow during the 20th century and considerably less than is taken out of it for human use today. Such a flow today would mean serious shortages, and serious water wars. "The Colorado River at 12 million acre-feet would be real ugly," says one water manager.

Unfortunately, global warming could make things even uglier. Last April, a month before Meko and Woodhouse published their latest results, a comprehensive study of climate models reported in *Science* predicted the Southwest's gradual descent into persistent Dust Bowl conditions by mid-century. Researchers at the National Oceanic and Atmospheric Administration (NOAA), meanwhile, have used some of the same models to project Colorado streamflow. In their simulations, which have been confirmed by others, the river never emerges from the current drought. Before mid-century, its flow falls to seven million acre-feet—around half the amount consumed today.

The wet 20th century, the wettest of the past millennium, the century when Americans built an incredible civilization in the desert, is over. Trees in the West are adjusting to the change, and not just in the width of their annual rings: In the recent drought they have been dying off and burning in wildfires at an unprecedented rate. For most people in the region, the news hasn't quite sunk in. Between 2000 and 2006 the seven states of the Colorado basin added five million people, a 10 percent population increase. Subdivisions continue to sprout in the desert, farther and farther from the cities whose own water supply is uncertain. Water managers are facing up to hard times ahead. "I look at the turn of the century as the defining moment when the New West began," says Pat Mulroy, head of the Southern Nevada Water Authority. "It's like the impact of global warming fell on us overnight."

In July 2007 a few dozen climate specialists gathered at Columbia University's Lamont-Doherty Earth Observatory to discuss the past and future of the world's drylands, especially the Southwest. Between sessions they took coffee and lunch outside, on a large sloping lawn above the Hudson River, which gathers as much water as the Colorado from a drainage area just over a twentieth the size. It was overcast and pleasantly cool for summer in New York. Phoenix was on its way to setting a record of 32 days in a single year with temperatures above 110 degrees. A scientist who had flown in from the West Coast reported that he had seen wildfires burning all over Nevada from his airplane window.

On the first morning, much of the talk was about medieval megadroughts. Scott Stine of California State University, East Bay, presented vivid evidence that they had extended beyond the Colorado River basin, well into California. Stine works in and around the Sierra Nevada, whose snows are the largest source of water for that heavily populated state. Some of the runoff drains into Mono Lake on the eastern flank of the Sierra. After Los Angeles began diverting the streams that feed Mono Lake in the 1940s, the lake's water level dropped 45 vertical feet.

In the late 1970s, tramping across the newly exposed shorelines, Stine found dozens of tree stumps, mostly cottonwood and Jeffrey pine, rooted in place. They were gnarled and ancient looking and encased in tufa—a whitish gray calcium carbonate crust that precipitates from the briny water of the lake. Clearly the trees had grown when a severe and long-lasting drought had lowered the lake and exposed the land where they had taken root; they had died when a return to a wetter climate in the

Sierra Nevada caused the lake to drown them. Their rooted remains were now exposed because Los Angeles had drawn the lake down.

Stine found drowned stumps in many other places in the Sierra Nevada. They all fell into two distinct generations, corresponding to two distinct droughts. The first had begun sometime before 900 and lasted over two centuries. There followed several extremely wet decades, not unlike those of the early 20th century. Then the next epic drought kicked in for 150 years, ending around 1350. Stine estimates that the runoff into Sierran lakes during the droughts must have been less than 60 percent of the modern average, and it may have been as low as 25 percent, for decades at a time. "What we have come to consider normal is profoundly wet," Stine said. "We're kidding ourselves if we think that's going to continue, with or without global warming."

No one is sure what caused the medieval megadroughts. Today Southwestern droughts follow the rhythm of La Niña, a periodic cooling of the eastern equatorial Pacific. La Niña alternates every few years with its warm twin, El Niño, and both make weather waves around the globe. A La Niña cooling of less than a degree Celsius was enough to trigger the recent drought, in part because it shifted the jet stream and the track of the winter storms northward, out of the Southwest. Richard Seager, of Lamont, and his colleagues have shown that all the western droughts in the historical record, including the Dust Bowl, can be explained by small but unusually persistent La Niñas. Though the evidence is slimmer, Seager thinks the medieval megadroughts too may have been caused by the tropical Pacific seesaw getting stuck in something like a perpetual La Niña.

The future, though, won't be governed by that kind of natural fluctuation alone. Thanks to our emissions of greenhouse gases, it will be subject as well to a global one-way trend toward higher temperatures. In one talk at Lamont, climate theorist Isaac Held, from NOAA's Geophysical Fluid Dynamics Laboratory in Princeton, gave two reasons why global warming seems almost certain to make the drylands drier. Both have to do with an atmospheric

As the West dries out, the landscape is transformed. Without cold winters to kill off their larvae, mountain pine beetles infest up to 90 percent of lodgepole pines in Colorado forests, like this one near Granby (left). The dead trees raise the risk of wildfires. In much of the West warmer, drier winters have reduced snowpack, a crucial water source. On California's Mount Shasta (right) a hiker traverses a snow patch diminished by milder temperatures.

circulation pattern called Hadley cells. At the Equator, warm, moist air rises, cools, sheds its moisture in tropical downpours, then spreads toward both Poles. In the subtropics, at latitudes of about 30 degrees, the dry air descends to the surface, where it sucks up moisture, creating the world's deserts—the Sahara, the deserts of Australia, and the arid lands of the Southwest. Surface winds export the moisture out of the dry subtropics to temperate and tropical latitudes. Global warming will intensify the whole process. The upshot is, the dry regions will get drier, and the wet regions will get wetter. "That's it," said Held. "There's nothing subtle here. Why do we need climate models to tell us that? Well, we really don't."

A second, subtler effect amplifies the drying. As the planet warms, the poleward edge of the Hadley cells, where the deserts are, expands a couple of degrees latitude farther toward each Pole. No one really knows what causes this

effect—but nearly all climate models predict it, making it what modelers call a robust result. Because the Southwest is right on the northern edge of the dry zone, a northward shift will plunge the region deeper into aridity.

As the meeting neared its close, Held and Seager stood out on the lawn, discussing Hadley cells and related matters through mouthfuls of coffee and doughnuts. The two men had lately become collaborators, and a few months before had published with colleagues the sobering *Science* paper analyzing the results of 19 different simulations done by climate modeling groups around the world. They then averaged all these results into an "ensemble."

The ensemble shows precipitation in the Southwest steadily declining over the next few decades, until by mid-century, Dust Bowl conditions are the norm. It does not show the Pacific locked in a perpetual La Niña. Rather, La Niñas would continue to happen as they do today (the present one is expected to continue at least through the winter of 2008), but against a background state that is more profoundly arid. According to the ensemble model, the descent into that state may already have started.

People are not yet suffering, but trees are. Forests in the West are dying, most impressively by burning. The damage done by wildfires in the United States, the vast majority of them in the West, has soared since the late 1980s. In 2006 nearly ten million acres were destroyed—an all-time record matched the very next year. With temperatures in the region up four degrees Farenheit over the past 30 years, spring is coming sooner to the western mountains. The snowpack—already diminished by drought—melts earlier in the year, drying the land and giving the wildfire season a jump start. As hotter summers encroach on autumn, the fires are ending later as well.

The fires are not only more frequent; they are also hotter and more damaging—though not entirely because of climate change. According to Tom Swetnam, director of the University of Arizona tree-ring lab, the root cause is the government's policy, adopted early in the 20th century, of trying to extinguish all wildfires. By studying sections cut from dead, thousand-year-old giant sequoias in the Sierra Nevada and from ponderosa pines all over Arizona and New Mexico, Swetnam discovered that most southwestern forests have always burned often—but at low intensity, with flames just a few feet high that raced through the grasses and the needles on the forest floor. The typical tree bears the marks of many such events, black scars where flames ate through the bark and perhaps even took a deep wedge out of the tree, but left it alive to heal its wound with new growth. Suppressing those natural fires has produced denser forests, with flammable litter piled up on the floor, and thickets of shrubs and young trees that act as fire ladders. When fires start now, they don't stay on the ground—they shoot up those ladders to the crowns of the trees. They blow thousand-acre holes in the forest and send mushroom clouds into the air.

One day last summer, Swetnam took a few visitors up Mount Lemmon, just north of Tucson, to see what the aftermath of such events looks like. In May 2002 the Bullock fire roared up the northeast slope of Mount Lemmon, consuming 30,000 acres. Firefighters stopped it at the Catalina Highway, protecting the village of Summerhaven. But the very next year, the Aspen fire started on the slope just below the village, destroying nearly half of the 700-odd houses in Summerhaven and burning 85,000 acres, all the way down to the outskirts of Tucson. The entire mountainside beyond the village remains covered with the gray skeletons of ponderosa pines, like one big blast zone. "Ponderosa pine is not adapted to these crown fires," Swetnam said, contemplating the site from the scenic overlook above the village. "It has heavy, wingless seeds that don't go very far. When you get a large hole like this, it will take hundreds of years to fill in from the edges."

Mount Lemmon's forests are also experiencing a slower, broader change. The Catalina Highway starts out flat, at an altitude of 2,500 feet in the Sonoran Desert, with its saguaros and strip malls. As the road leaves the last of Tucson behind, it climbs steeply through the whole range of southwestern woodland ecosystems—first scrub oak, then piñon and juniper, then ponderosa pine and other conifers, until finally, after less than an hour and a climb of 7,000 feet, you reach the spruce and fir trees on the cool peak. There is a small ski area there, the southernmost in the United States, and its days are certainly numbered.

As Swetnam explained, the mountain is one of an archipelago of "sky islands" spread across southeastern Arizona, New Mexico, Texas, and into Mexico—mountains isolated from one another by a sea of desert or grassland. Like isles in the ocean, these islands are populated in part by endemics—species that live nowhere else. The sky-island endemics are cool- and wet-loving species that have taken refuge on the mountaintops since the last ice age. They are things like the corkbark fir, or the endangered red squirrel that lives only on nearby Mount Graham. Their future is as bleak as that of the ski area. "They'll be picked off the top," said Swetnam. "The islands are shrinking. The aridity is advancing upslope."

All over the Southwest, a wholesale change in the landscape is under way. Piñons and scrubbier, more drought-resistant junipers have long been partners in the low woodlands that clothe much of the region. But the piñons are dying off. From 2002 to 2004, 2.5 million acres turned to rust in the Four Corners region alone. The immediate cause of death was often bark beetles, which are also devastating other conifers. The Forest Service estimates that in 2003, beetles infested 14 million acres of piñon, ponderosa, lodgepole pine, and Douglas fir in the American West.

Bark beetles tend to attack trees that are already stressed or dying from drought. "They can smell it," says Craig Allen, a landscape ecologist at Bandelier National Monument in the Jemez Mountains of New Mexico. Global climate change may be permanently teasing the piñons and junipers apart, and replacing piñon-juniper woodland with something new. At Bandelier, Allen has observed that junipers, along with shrubs such as wavyleaf oak and mountain mahogany, now dominate the beetle-ravaged landscape: pockets of green gradually spreading beneath a shroud of dead piñons.

Just as there are global climate models, there are global models that forecast how vegetation will change as the climate warms. They predict that on roughly half of Earth's surface, something different will be growing in 2100 than is growing there now. The models are not good, however, at projecting what scientists call "transient dynamics"—the damage done by droughts, fires, and beetle infestations that will actually accomplish the transformation. Large trees cannot simply migrate to higher latitudes and altitudes; they are rooted to the spot. "What happens to what's there now?" Allen wonders. "Stuff dies quicker than it grows."

Over the next few decades, Allen predicts, people in the Southwest will be seeing a lot of death in the old landscapes while waiting for the new ones to be born. "This is a dilemma

Sequoias may not survive in Sequoia National Park. What do you do? Do you irrigate these things? Or do you let a 2,000-year-old tree die?

for the Park Service," he says. "The projections are that Joshua trees may not survive in Joshua Tree National Park. Sequoias may not survive in Sequoia National Park. What do you do? Do you irrigate these things? Or do you let a 2,000-year-old tree die?"

While the trees die, the subdivisions proliferate. "Our job was to entice people to move to the West, and we did a darn good job," says Terry Fulp, who manages water releases at Hoover Dam. The federal Bureau of Reclamation built the dam in the 1930s primarily to supply the vegetable farms of the Imperial Valley and only secondarily to supply the residents of Los Angeles. Farmers had first claim to the water—they still do—but there was plenty to go around. "At Lake Mead, we basically gave the water away," says Fulp. "At the time, it made perfect sense. There was no one out here." After Reclamation built Hoover and the other big dams, more people came to the desert than anyone ever expected. Few of them are farmers anymore, and farming, crucial as it is to human welfare, is now a small part of the economy. But it still uses around three-quarters of the water in the Colorado River and elsewhere in the Southwest.

In the wet 1920s, as the dam was being planned, seven states drew up the Colorado River Compact to divvy up 15 million acre-feet of its water. California, Nevada, and Arizona—the so-called Lower Basin states—would get half, plus any surplus from the Upper Basin states of Wyoming, Colorado, New Mexico, and Utah. The compact also acknowledged Mexico's rights to the water. Surpluses were almost always on hand, because the Upper Basin states have never fully used the 7.5 million acre-feet they are entitled to under the compact. They are only entitled to use it, in fact, if in so doing they don't prevent the Lower Basin states from getting their 7.5 million—the compact is unfair that way. But in the wet 20th century, it didn't seem to matter.

In 1999 both Lake Mead and Lake Powell—created in 1963 upstream of Lake Mead to

A viable desert home during a long wet spell may be uninhabitable when the rains stop. The ancient Anasazi created a flourishing culture in New Mexico's Chaco Canyon, epitomized by Pueblo Bonito (left). Then prolonged drought hit the region in 1130. By the time it ended 30 years later, the Anasazi were gone. Sprawling cities in the present-day Southwest like Scottsdale (right) grew by the millions during half a century of above-average rainfall. But with no end to the present drying trend in sight, the region faces an uncertain future.

ensure that the Upper Basin would have enough water even in drought years to meet its obligation to the Lower Basin—were nearly full, with 50 million acre-feet between them. Two years later, representatives of the states in the basin completed long and difficult negotiations with the Bureau of Reclamation on new guidelines for dividing up the surpluses from Lake Mead. Then came the drought. Both lakes are now only half full. "Those guidelines are almost a joke now," says the Southern Nevada Water Authority's Pat Mulroy. "All of a sudden, seven states that had spent years in surplus discussions had to turn on a dime and start discussing shortages."

Since the Hoover Dam was built, there has never been a water shortage on the Colorado, never a day when there was simply not enough water in Lake Mead to meet all the downstream allocations. Drought, and a realistic understanding of the past, have made such a day seem more imminent. Under the pressure of the drought, the seven Colorado basin states have agreed for the first time on how to share prospective shortages. Arizona will bear almost all the pain at first, because the Central Arizona Project, which

came on line in 1993, has junior rights. Nevada will lose only a small percentage of its allotment.

Meanwhile California would give up nothing, at least until Lake Mead falls below 1,025 feet, nearly 200 feet below "full pool." At that point, negotiations would resume. According to Bureau of Reclamation calculations, a return of the 12th-century drought would force Lake Mead well below that level, perhaps even to "dead pool" at 895 feet—the level at which water no longer flows out of the lake without pumping. Reclamation officials consider this extremely unlikely. But their calculations do not take into account the impact of global warming.

Every utility in the Southwest now preaches conservation and sustainability, sometimes very forcefully. Las Vegas has prohibited new front lawns, limited the size of back ones, and offers people two dollars a square foot to tear existing ones up and replace them with desert plants. Between 2002 and 2006, the Vegas metro area actually managed to reduce its total consumption of water by around 20 percent, even though its population had increased substantially. Albuquerque too has cut its water use. But every water manager also knows that, as one puts it, "at some point, growth is going to catch up to you."

Looking for new long-term sources of supply, many water managers turn their lonely eyes to the Pacific, or to deep, briny aquifers that had always seemed unusable. Last August, El Paso inaugurated a new desalination plant that will allow the city to tap one such aquifer. The same month, the Bureau of Reclamation opened a new research center devoted to desalination in Ala-mogordo, New Mexico. The cost of desalination has dropped dramatically—it's now around four dollars per thousand gallons, or as little as $1,200 per acre-foot—but that is still considerably more than the 50 cents per acre-foot that the Bureau of Reclamation charges municipal utilities for water from Lake Mead, or the zero dollars it charges irrigation districts. The environmental impacts of desalination are also uncertain—there is always a concentrated brine to be disposed of. Nevertheless, a large desalination plant is being planned in San Diego County. In Las Vegas, Mulroy envisions one day paying for such a plant on the coast of California or Mexico, in exchange for a portion of either's share of the water in Lake Mead. "The problem is, if there's nothing in Lake Mead, there's nothing to exchange," she says.

A more obvious solution for cities facing shortages is to buy irrigation water from farmers. In 2003 the Imperial Irrigation District was pressured into selling 200,000 of its three million acre-feet of Colorado water to San Diego, as part of an overall deal to get California to stop exceeding its allotment. San Diego paid nearly $300 per acre-foot for water that the farmers in the Imperial Valley get virtually for free. The government favors such market mechanisms, says the Bureau of Reclamation's Terry Fulp, "so people who really want the water get it." At that price, the irrigation water in the Imperial Valley is worth nearly as much as its entire agricultural revenue, which is around a billion dollars a year.

> The West was built by dreamers.... As the climate that underpinned **that expansive vision vanishes,** the vision needed to replace it has not yet emerged.

But not everyone favors drying up farms so that more water will be available for subdivisions. The valley is one of the poorest regions in California, yet the richest farmers stand to benefit most from the sale. Many more people fear the loss of jobs and, ultimately, of a whole way of life.

The West was built by dreamers. The men who conceived Hoover Dam were, in the words beneath a flagpole on the Nevada side, "inspired by a vision of lonely lands made fruitful." As the climate that underpinned that expansive vision vanishes, the vision needed to replace it has not yet emerged. In a drying climate, the human ecosystems established in a wetter one will have to change—die and be replaced by new ones. The people in the Southwest face the same uncertain future, the same question, as their forests: What happens to the stuff that's there now?

In the second half of the 13th century, as a drying trend set in, people who had lived for centuries at Mesa Verde moved down off the mesa into the canyons. They built villages around water sources, under overhangs high up in the walls of the cliffs, and climbed back up the cliffs to farm; their handholds in the rock are still visible. Some of the villages were fortified, because apparently their position on a cliff face was not defense enough. Those cliff dwellings, abandoned now for seven centuries but still intact and eerily beautiful, are what attract so many visitors today. But they are certainly not the product of an expansive, outward-looking civilization. They are the product of a civilization in a crouch, waiting to get hit again. In that period, the inhabitants of the Mesa Verde region began carving petroglyphs suggesting violent conflict between men armed with shields, bows and arrows, and clubs. And then, in the last two or three decades of the century, right when the tree rings record one of the most severe droughts in the region, the people left. They never came back.

Discussion Questions

- Why is the distinction between "complacent" and "sensitive" trees so important?

- Explain the implications of the comment "You really need a catastrophe to get people's attention" (51).

- How did a century of measurements fail to provide an adequate picture of the West's dry spells?

- What benefits do we gain from taking into consideration the information trees offer about climate changes before the 20th century?

Writing Activities

- What does the broader picture presented in this article suggest to us about the wisdom of modern human development across the West? Write an essay that evaluates our past decisions in light of what we can expect in the future based on historical evidence.

- It may not be realistic to imagine abandoning our western cities and towns in the face of a megadrought. In that case, what can be done to survive one, given the way we have already structured our communities and economies in the region? Write an essay in which you analyze the problem and its degree of urgency, and propose some alternatives that might allow western communities to thrive in an increasingly dry environment. If you do not see viable alternatives to the way of life already established there, present a realistic vision of the future for this region.

- Research the frequency of wildfires in the West and Southwest since the 2008 publication of this article. Have the predictions it makes been confirmed or disproved by subsequent events? Write an essay that combines recent evidence with examples presented in this article, and from this evidence build an argument for rethinking some of the assumptions upon which the cities and towns of the west have been developed, taking into account the facts as you see them.

- Write an essay that compares and/or contrasts the extent Westerners have benefitted from the exploitation of rivers in the region, and the damage done to these water supplies by overuse.

Collaborative Activities

- Working together, compile a list of compelling questions that could be presented to a regional planning board to help shape a plan for a future in which free and unlimited water from the Colorado River and its tributaries is no longer available.

- Work with a partner to identify and then classify the kinds of problems presented in Kunzig's article. Compare your group's classifications with those of another group and identify and discuss differences in your choices.

THE BIG MELT

The glacial ice of the Tibetan Plateau is the source of some of the most notable rivers in human history. The scope of the threat to this source from climate change is almost unimaginable, yet the impact is already being felt across the Asian continent.

As you read "The Big Melt" consider the following questions:

- How important is normal seasonal glacial melt in the life of the region?
- What changes in ice and water patterns have been observed over the past few decades, and what is the impact on various communities, both rural and urban, today?
- What is the extent of the threat posed by the loss of glacial ice on the Tibetan Plateau, and how is the problem being addressed?

THE BIG MELT

Photographs by Jonas Bendiksen

Bangladeshis in Sirajganj haul boatloads of bagged sand to reinforce a levee eroded by the flooding of the Jamuna River. If melting ice swells the rivers, such stopgap fixes may become more common.

GLACIERS IN THE HIGH HEART OF ASIA FEED
ITS GREATEST RIVERS,

LIFELINES FOR TWO BILLION PEOPLE.
NOW THE ICE AND SNOW ARE DIMINISHING.

The gods must be furious. It's the only explanation that makes sense to Jia Son, a Tibetan farmer surveying the catastrophe unfolding above his village in China's mountainous Yunnan Province. "We've upset the natural order," the devout, 52-year-old Buddhist says. "And now the gods are punishing us."

On a warm summer afternoon, Jia Son has hiked a mile and a half up the gorge that Mingyong Glacier has carved into sacred Mount "Kawagebo, looming 22,113 feet high in the clouds above. There's no sign of ice, just a river roiling with silt-laden melt. For more than a century, ever since its tongue lapped at the edge of Mingyong village, the glacier has retreated like a dying serpent recoiling into its lair. Its pace has accelerated over the past decade, to more than a football field every year—a distinctly unglacial rate for an ancient ice mass.

"This all used to be ice ten years ago," Jia Son says, as he scrambles across the scree and brush. He points out a yak trail etched into the slope some 200 feet above the valley bottom.

> **W**e've upset a natural order, and now **the Gods are punishing us.**

"The glacier sometimes used to cover that trail, so we had to lead our animals over the ice to get to the upper meadows."

Around a bend in the river, the glacier's snout finally comes into view: It's a deathly shade of black, permeated with pulverized rock and dirt. The water from this ice, once so pure it served in rituals as a symbol of Buddha himself, is now too loaded with sediment for the villagers to drink. For nearly a mile the glacier's once smooth surface is ragged and cratered like the skin of a leper. There are glimpses of blue-green ice within the fissures, but the cracks themselves signal trouble. "The beast is sick and wasting away," Jia Son says. "If our sacred glacier cannot survive, how can we?"

It is a question that echoes around the globe, but nowhere more urgently than across the vast swath of Asia that draws its water from the "roof of the world." This geologic colossus—the highest and largest plateau on the planet, ringed by its tallest mountains—covers an

Adapted from "The Big Melt" by Brook Larmer:
National Geographic Magazine, April 2010.

area greater than western Europe, at an average altitude of more than two miles. With nearly 37,000 glaciers on the Chinese side alone, the Tibetan Plateau and its surrounding arc of mountains contain the largest volume of ice outside the polar regions. This ice gives birth to Asia's largest and most legendary rivers, from the Yangtze and the Yellow to the Mekong and the Ganges—rivers that over the course of history have nurtured civilizations, inspired religions, and sustained ecosystems. Today they are lifelines for some of Asia's most densely settled areas, from the arid plains of Pakistan to the thirsty metropolises of northern China 3,000 miles away. All told, some two billion people in more than a dozen countries—nearly a third of the world's population—depend on rivers fed by the snow and ice of the plateau region.

But a crisis is brewing on the roof of the world, and it rests on a curious paradox: For all its seeming might and immutability, this geologic expanse is more vulnerable to climate change than almost anywhere else on Earth. The Tibetan Plateau as a whole is heating up twice as fast as the global average of 1.3°F over the past century—and in some places even faster. These warming rates, unprecedented for at least two millennia, are merciless on the glaciers, whose rare confluence of high altitudes and low latitudes make them especially sensitive to shifts in climate.

For thousands of years the glaciers have formed what Lonnie Thompson, a glaciologist at Ohio State University, calls "Asia's fresh water bank account"—an immense storehouse whose buildup of new ice and snow (deposits) has historically offset its annual runoff (withdrawals). Glacial melt plays its most vital role before and after the rainy season, when it supplies a greater portion of the flow in every river from the Yangtze (which irrigates more than half of China's rice) to the Ganges and the Indus (key to the agricultural heartlands of India and Pakistan).

> **F**ullscale **glacier shrinkage is inevitable. It will lead to ecological catastrophe.**

But over the past half century, the balance has been lost, perhaps irrevocably. Of the 680 glaciers Chinese scientists monitor closely on the Tibetan Plateau, 95 percent are shedding more ice than they're adding, with the heaviest losses on its southern and eastern edges. "These glaciers are not simply retreating," Thompson says. "They're losing mass from the surface down."

The ice cover in this portion of the plateau has shrunk more than 6 percent since the 1970s—and the damage is still greater in Tajikistan and northern India, with 35 percent and 20 percent declines respectively over the past five decades.

The rate of melting is not uniform, and a number of glaciers in the Karakoram Range on the western edge of the plateau are actually advancing. This anomaly may result from increases in snowfall in the higher latitude—and therefore colder—Karakorams, where snow and ice are less vulnerable to small temperature increases. The gaps in scientific knowledge are still great, and in the Tibetan Plateau they are deepened by the region's remoteness and political sensitivity—as well as by the inherent complexities of climate science.

Though scientists argue about the rate and cause of glacial retreat, most don't deny that it's happening. And they believe the worst may be yet to come. The more dark areas that are exposed by melting, the more sunlight is absorbed than reflected, causing temperatures to rise faster. (Some climatologists believe this warming feedback loop could intensify the Asian monsoon, triggering more violent storms and flooding in places such as Bangladesh and Myanmar.) If current trends hold, Chinese scientists believe that 40 percent of the plateau's glaciers could disappear by 2050. "Full-scale glacier shrinkage is inevitable," says Yao Tandong, a glaciologist at China's Institute of Tibetan Plateau Research. "And it will lead to ecological catastrophe."

The potential impacts extend far beyond the glaciers. On the Tibetan Plateau, especially its dry northern flank, people are already affected by a warmer climate. The grasslands and wetlands are deteriorating, and the permafrost that feeds them with spring and summer melt is retreating to higher elevations. Thousands of lakes have dried up. Desert now covers about one-sixth of the plateau, and in places sand dunes lap across the highlands like waves in a yellow sea. The herders who once thrived here are running out of options.

Along the plateau's southern edge, by contrast, many communities are coping with too much water. In alpine villages like Mingyong, the glacial melt has swelled rivers, with welcome side effects: expanded croplands and longer growing seasons. But such benefits often hide deeper costs. In Mingyong, surging meltwater has carried away topsoil; elsewhere, excess runoff has been blamed for more frequent flooding and landslides. In the mountains from Pakistan to Bhutan, thousands of glacial lakes have formed, many potentially unstable. Among the more dangerous is Imja Tsho, at 16,400 feet on the trail to Nepal's Island Peak. Fifty years ago the lake didn't exist; today, swollen by melt, it is a mile long and 300 feet deep. If it ever burst through its loose wall of moraine, it would drown the Sherpa villages in the valley below.

This situation—too much water, too little water—captures, in miniature, the trajectory of the overall crisis. Even if melting glaciers provide an abundance of water in the short run, they portend a frightening endgame: the eventual depletion of Asia's greatest rivers. Nobody can predict exactly when the glacier retreat will translate into a sharp drop in runoff. Whether it happens in 10, 30, or 50 years depends on local conditions, but the collateral damage across the region could be devastating. Along with acute water and electricity shortages, experts predict a plunge in food production, widespread migration in the face of ecological changes, even conflicts between Asian powers.

The nomads' tent is a pinprick of white against a canvas of green and brown. There is no other sign of human existence on the 14,000-foot-high prairie that seems to extend to the end of the world. As a vehicle rattles toward the tent, two young men emerge, their long black hair horizontal in the wind. Ba O and his brother Tsering are part of an unbroken line of Tibetan nomads who for at least a thousand years have led their herds to summer grazing grounds near the headwaters of the Yangtze and Yellow Rivers.

Inside the tent, Ba O's wife tosses patties of dried yak dung onto the fire while her four-year-old son plays with a spool of sheep's wool. The family matriarch, Lu Ji, churns yak milk into cheese, rocking back and forth in a hypnotic rhythm. Behind her are two weathered Tibetan chests topped with a small Buddhist shrine: a red prayer wheel, a couple of smudged Tibetan texts, and several yak butter candles whose flames are never allowed to go out, "This is the way we've always done things," Ba O says. "And we don't want that to change."

But it may be too late. The grasslands are dying out, as decades of warming temperatures—exacerbated by overgrazing—turn prairie into desert. Watering holes are drying up, and now, instead of traveling a short distance to find summer grazing for their herds, Ba O and his family must trek more than 30 miles across the high plateau. Even there the grass is meager. "It used to grow so high you could lose a sheep in it," Ba O says. "Now it doesn't reach above their hooves." The family's herd has dwindled from 500 animals to 120. The next step seems inevitable: selling their remaining livestock and moving into a government resettlement camp.

Across Asia the response to climate-induced threats has mostly been slow and piecemeal, as if governments would prefer to leave it up to the industrialized countries that pumped the greenhouse gases into the atmosphere in the first place. There are exceptions. In Ladakh, a bone-dry region in northern India and Pakistan that relies entirely on melting ice and snow, a retired civil *(Continued on page 68)*

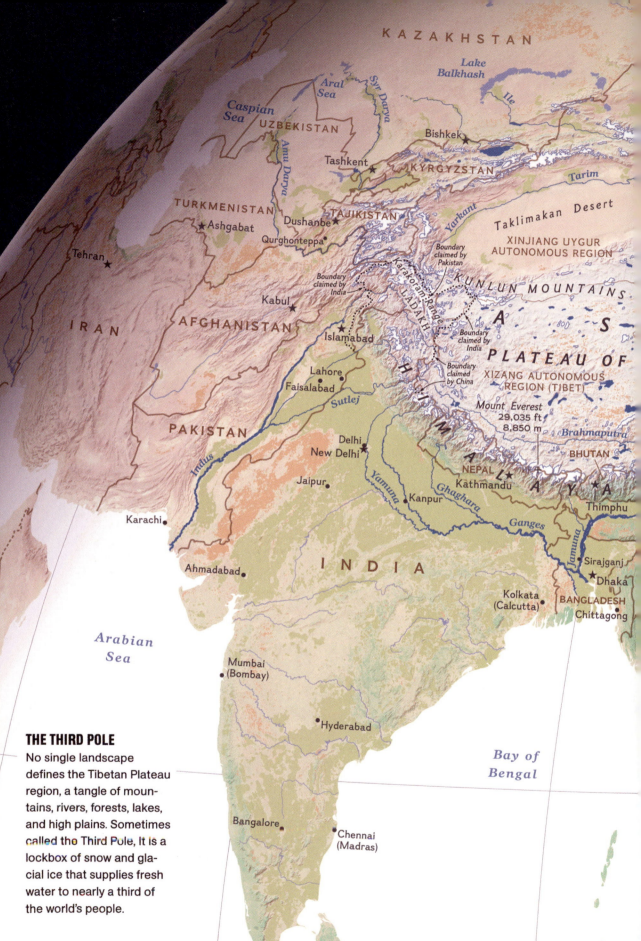

KAZAKHSTAN

Lake Balkhash

Ile

Aral Sea

Caspian Sea

Syr Darya

UZBEKISTAN

Bishkek ★

Tashkent ★

KYRGYZSTAN

Tarim

Amu Darya

TURKMENISTAN

★ Ashgabat

Dushanbe ★

Qurghonteppa •

TAJIKISTAN

Yarkant

Taklimakan Desert

XINJIANG UYGUR AUTONOMOUS REGION

Tehran ★

Boundary claimed by Pakistan

KUNLUN MOUNTAINS

Karakoram Range

LADAKH

Boundary claimed by India

A S I

800

IRAN

AFGHANISTAN

Kabul •

Islamabad ★

Boundary claimed by India

Boundary claimed by China

PLATEAU OF

XIZANG AUTONOMOUS REGION (TIBET)

Lahore •

Faisalabad •

Sutlej

H I M A L A Y A

Mount Everest 29,035 ft 8,850 m

Brahmaputra

BHUTAN

PAKISTAN

Indus

Delhi ★
New Delhi ★

Jaipur •

Yamuna

NEPAL ★

Kathmandu ★

Thimphu ★

Karachi •

Kanpur •

Ghaghara

Ganges

Jamuna

Sirajganj •

Dhaka ●

Ahmadabad •

I N D I A

Kolkata (Calcutta) •

BANGLADESH

Chittagong •

Arabian Sea

Mumbai (Bombay) •

Hyderabad •

Bay of Bengal

THE THIRD POLE

No single landscape
defines the Tibetan Plateau
region, a tangle of moun-
tains, rivers, forests, lakes,
and high plains. Sometimes
called the Third Pole, it is a
lockbox of snow and gla-
cial ice that supplies fresh
water to nearly a third of
the world's people.

Bangalore •

Chennai (Madras) •

SRI LANKA

RUSSIA

MONGOLIA

Ulaanbaatar

Lop Nur

QINGHAI

Madoi

Lanzhou

TIBET

I A

Baotou

Beijing

Taiyuan

Jinan

Yellow

Xian

Zhengzhou

C H I N A

GRAND CANAL

Yellow
Sea

Chengdu

Yangtze

Wuhan

Nanjing

Shanghai

Hangzhou

Mount
Kawagebo
22,113 ft
6,740 m

Chongqing

Nanchang

30°

Mingyong

Boundary
claimed by
China

YUNNAN

Irrawaddy

MYANMAR
(BURMA)

Salween

Nay Pyi Taw

LAOS

Hanoi

Guangzhou

Hong Kong

Taipei

TAIWAN

Vientiane

Mekong

Yangon
(Rangoon)

THAILAND

V
I
E
T
N
A
M

South
China
Sea

15°N

Bangkok

CAMBODIA

Forest

Cropland

Grassland

Glacier

SCALE VARIES IN THIS PERSPECTIVE. DISTANCE FROM
NEW DELHI TO DHAKA IS 890 MILES (1,432 KILOMETERS).

© 2010 ALLAN CARTOGRAPHY INC/National Geographic
Image Collection

Phnom Penh

Ho Chi Minh City

(Continued from page 65) engineer named Chewang Norphel has built "artificial glaciers"—simple stone embankments that trap and freeze glacial melt, in the fall for use in the early spring growing season. Nepal is developing a remote monitoring system to gauge when glacial lakes are in danger of bursting, as well as the technology to drain them. Even in places facing destructive monsoonal flooding, such as Bangladesh, "floating schools" in the delta enable kids to continue their education—on boats.

But nothing compares to the campaign in China, which has less water than Canada but 40 times more people. In the vast desert in the Xinjiang region, just north of the Tibetan Plateau, China aims to build 59 reservoirs to capture and save glacial runoff. Across Tibet, artillery batteries have been installed to launch rain-inducing silver iodide into the clouds. In Qinghai the government is blocking off degraded grasslands in hopes they can be nurtured back to health. In areas where grasslands have already turned to scrub desert, bales of wire fencing are rolled out over the last remnants of plant life to prevent them from blowing away.

It is not yet noon in Delhi, just 180 miles south of the Himalayan glaciers. But in the narrow corridors of Nehru Camp, a slum in this city of 16 million, the blast furnace of the north Indian summer has already sent temperatures soaring past 105 degrees Fahrenheit. Chaya, the 25-year-old wife of a fortune-teller, has spent seven hours joining the mad scramble for water that, even today, defines life in this heaving metropolis—and offers a taste of what the depletion of Tibet's water and ice portends.

Chaya's day began long before sunrise, when she and her five children fanned out in the darkness, armed with plastic jugs of every size. After daybreak, the rumor of a tap with running water sent her stumbling in a panic through the slum's narrow corridors. Now, with her containers still empty and the sun blazing overhead, she has returned home for a moment's rest. Asked if she's eaten anything today, she laughs: "We haven't even had any tea yet."

Suddenly cries erupt— a water truck has been spotted. Chaya leaps up and joins the human torrent in the street A dozen boys swarm onto a blue tanker, jamming hoses in and siphoning the water out. Below, shouting women jostle for position with their containers. In six minutes the tanker is empty. Chaya arrived too late and must move on to chase the next rumor of water.

Delhi's water demand already exceeds supply by more than 300 million gallons a day, a shortfall worsened by inequitable distribution and a leaky infrastructure that loses an estimated 40 percent of the water. More than two-thirds of the city's water is pulled from the Yamuna and the Ganges, rivers fed by Himalayan ice. If that ice disappears, the future will almost certainly be worse. "We are facing an unsustainable situation," says Diwan Singh, a Delhi environmental activist. "Soon—not in thirty years but in five to ten—there will be an exodus because of the lack of water."

The tension already seethes. In the clogged alleyway around one of Nehru Camp's last functioning taps, which run for one hour a day, a man punches a woman who cut in line, leaving a purple welt on her face. "We wake up every morning fighting over water," says Kamal Bhate, a local astrologer watching the melee. This one dissolves into shouting and finger-pointing, but the brawls can be deadly. In a nearby slum a teenage boy was recently beaten to death for cutting in line.

As the rivers dwindle, the conflicts could spread. India, China, and Pakistan all face pressure to boost food production to keep up with their huge and growing populations. But climate change and diminishing water supplies could reduce cereal yields in South Asia by 5 percent within three decades. "We're going to see rising tensions over shared water resources, including political disputes between farmers, between farmers and cities, and between human and ecological demands for water," says Peter Gleick, a water expert and president of the Pacific Institute in Oakland, California. "And I believe more of these tensions will lead to violence."

The real challenge will be to prevent water conflicts from spilling across borders. There is already a growing sense of alarm in Central Asia over the prospect that poor but glacier-heavy nations (Tajikistan, Kyrgyzstan) may one day restrict the flow of water to their parched but oil-rich neighbors (Uzbekistan, Kazakhstan, Turkmenistan). In the future, peace between Pakistan and India may hinge as much on water as on nuclear weapons, for the two countries must share the glacier-dependent Indus.

The biggest question mark hangs over China, which controls the sources of the region's major rivers. Its damming of the Mekong has sparked anger downstream in Indochina. If Beijing follows through on tentative plans to divert the Brahmaputra, it could provoke its rival, India, in the very region where the two countries fought a war in 1962.

Fatalism may be a natural response to forces that seem beyond our control. But Jia Son, the Tibetan farmer watching Mingyong Glacier shrink, believes that every action counts— good or bad, large or small. Pausing on the mountain trail, he makes a guilty confession. The melting ice, he says, may be his fault.

When Jia Son first noticed the rising temperatures—an unfamiliar trickle of sweat down his back about a decade ago—he figured it was a gift from the gods. Winter soon lost some of its brutal sting. The glacier began releasing its water earlier in the summer, and for the first time in memory villagers had the luxury of two harvests a year.

Then came the Chinese tourists, a flood of city dwellers willing to pay locals to take them up to see the glacier. The Han tourists don't always respect Buddhist traditions; in their gleeful hollers to provoke an icefall, they seem unaware of the calamity that has befallen the glacier. Still, they have turned a poor village into one of the region's wealthiest, "Life is much easier now," says Jia Son, whose simple farmhouse, like all in the village, has a television and government-subsidized satellite dish. "But maybe our greed has made Kawagebo angry."

He is referring to the temperamental deity above his village. One of the holiest mountains in Tibetan Buddhism, Kawagebo has never been conquered, and locals believe its summit—and its glacier—should remain untouched. When a Sino-Japanese expedition tried to scale the peak in 1991, an avalanche near the top of the glacier killed all 17 climbers. Jia Son remains convinced the deaths were not an accident but an act of divine retribution.

Could Mingyong's retreat be another sign of Kawagebo's displeasure?

Jia Son is taking no chances. Every year he embarks on a 15-day pilgrimage around Kawagebo to show his deepening Buddhist devotion. He no longer hunts animals or cuts down trees. As part of a government program, he has also given up a parcel of land to be reforested. His family still participates in the village's tourism cooperative, but Jia Son makes a point of telling visitors about the glacier's spiritual significance. "Nothing will get better," he says, "until we get rid of our materialistic thinking."

It's a simple pledge, perhaps, one that hardly seems enough to save the glaciers of the Tibetan Plateau—and stave off the water crisis that seems sure to follow. But here, in the shadow of one of the world's fastest retreating glaciers, this lone farmer has begun, in his own small way, to restore the balance.

Discussion Questions

- In what ways does the "curious paradox" mentioned on page 64 demand a new way of thinking about the Tibetan Plateau?

- Explain Thompson's metaphor describing the Tibetan Plateau's glaciers as "Asia's freshwater bank account" and discuss the implications relating to observed changes in the region's ice.

- How do warmer climates hide the scope of the crisis?

- Considering scientists' inability to predict when essential runoff from glaciers will a reach critical low point, how might this complicate efforts to address the problem?

Writing Activities

- Larmer refers to the rivers that flow from the Tibetan Plateau glaciers (Yangtze, Yellow, Mekong, and Ganges) as "Asia's largest and most legendary rivers," which have "nurtured civilizations, inspired religions, and sustained ecosystems." Analyze the parallel that the author draws between the cultural, environmental, and historical significance of these rivers and their roles as "lifelines" for one third of the human population.

- Write an essay that compares or contrasts the threats described in "The Big Melt" with those examined in "The Drying of the West."

- Examine the Tibetan farmer's interpretation of the changing world he lives in and his personal response to the problem as he sees it. Summarize the reasons why, in his worldview, the glacier is retreating, and then offer your own observations or interpretation of what has caused the crisis, arguing for or against the idea that an individual's actions can help "restore the balance" that has been lost.

- What measures can be taken to prevent water conflicts between nations? Write an essay that proposes some reasonable steps that can be taken now to help reduce tension in the face of large-scale and permanent shortages of water across Asian countries.

Collaborative Activities

- How would you rate the responses of various nations who are impacted directly by the loss of glacial ice in the Tibetan Plateau? Work in a small group to explore each other's views on the approaches taken so far. Where do they fall short or seem to take strong initiative? Which responses do you consider adequate, and which inadequate? List the factors that contribute to "slow and piecemeal" responses, and discuss the options available.

- Working in a small group, assess the scope of climate-related threats in Asia and the options available today to address the crisis. Compare views on what roles Europe, the Americas, and Canada have played in causing the problem, and discuss ways that the international community should contribute to its solutions.

THE END OF PLENTY

Joel K. Bourne, Jr. presents a somewhat bleak picture of a burgeoning global population likely to suffer from widespread hunger. Pointing to some of the primary causes of a potential food crisis of unprecedented proportions, he examines the problem in terms of limited resources, misapplied or unhealthy methods of agriculture, and the effects of climate change.

As you read "The End of Plenty," consider the following questions:

- What are the fundamental differences between one "green revolution" and another?
- What is meant by a "perpetual food crisis"?
- How does climate change contribute to large-scale food shortages?
- How and why have established methods of agriculture failed to keep up with the needs of the world's population, particularly in poor countries?

EGYPT

Stung by soaring food prices, angry Egyptians throng a kiosk selling government-subsidized bread near the Great Pyramid at Giza. Across the globe, rising demand and flat supplies have rekindled the old debate over whether production can keep up with population.

THE END OF PLENTY

SPECIAL REPORT:
THE GLOBAL FOOD CRISIS

Photographs by John Stanmeyer

BANGLADESH

A woman sweeps a harvested rice field, gleaning leftover grains to feed her family. One of the world's largest consumers of rice, Bangladesh needs more each year to feed its burgeoning population. A near-doubling of rice prices over the past two years—exacerbated by flooding and a major cyclone that devastated crops in 2007—brought the nation's total number of starving people to 35 million.

WE'VE BEEN CONSUMING MORE FOOD THAN FARMERS HAVE BEEN PRODUCING FOR MOST OF THE PAST DECADE. WHAT WILL IT TAKE TO GROW MORE?

It is the simplest, most natural of acts, akin to breathing and walking upright. We sit down at the dinner table, pick up a fork, and take a juicy bite, oblivious to the double helping of global ramifications on our plate. Our beef comes from Iowa, fed by Nebraska corn. Our grapes come from Chile, our bananas from Honduras, our olive oil from Sicily, our apple juice—not from Washington State but all the way from China. Modern society has relieved us of the burden of growing, harvesting, even preparing our daily bread, in exchange for the burden of simply paying for it. Only when prices rise do we take notice. And the consequences of our inattention are profound.

Last year the skyrocketing cost of food was a wake-up call for the planet. Between 2005 and the summer of 2008, the price of wheat and corn tripled, and the price of rice climbed five-fold, spurring food riots in nearly two dozen countries and pushing 75 million more people into poverty. But unlike previous shocks driven by short-term food shortages, this price spike came in a year when the world's farmers reaped a record grain crop. This time,

> **Only when prices rise do we take notice. And the consequences of our inattention are profound.**

the high prices were a symptom of a larger problem tugging at the strands of our worldwide food web, one that's not going away anytime soon. Simply put: For most of the past decade, the world has been consuming more food than it has been producing. After years of drawing down stockpiles, in 2007 the world saw global carryover stocks fall to 61 days of global consumption, the second lowest on record.

"Agricultural productivity growth is only one to two percent a year," warned Joachim von Braun, director general of the International Food Policy Research Institute in Washington, D.C., at the height of the crisis. "This is too low to meet population growth and increased demand."

High prices are the ultimate signal that demand is outstripping supply, that there is simply not enough food to go around. Such agflation hits the poorest billion people on the planet the hardest, since they typically spend 50 to 70 percent of their income on food. Even though prices have *(Continued on page 78)*

(Continued on page 78)

Adapted from "The End of Plenty" by Joel K. Bourne Jr.: National Geographic Magazine, June 2009.

U.S.A.

Jason Hinson, a sixth-generation corn farmer near Kingston, Iowa, keeps an eye on his auger as he unloads his combine on the fly. Federal mandates for corn-based ethanol soaked up 30 percent of the 2008 U.S. crop, helping send corn prices over eight dollars a bushel last year—triple the 2005 price. As long as energy prices remain high, biofuels will compete with food for land and water across the globe.

(Continued from page 75) fallen with the imploding world economy, they are still near record highs, and the underlying problems of low stockpiles, rising population, and flattening yield growth remain. Climate change—with its hotter growing seasons and increasing water scarcity—is projected to reduce future harvests in much of the world, raising the specter of what some scientists are now calling a perpetual food crisis.

So what is a hot, crowded, and hungry world to do?

That's the question von Braun and his colleagues at the Consultative Group on International Agricultural Research are wrestling with right now. This is the group of world-renowned agricultural research centers that helped more than double the world's average yields of corn, rice, and wheat between the mid-1950s and the mid-1990s, an achievement so staggering it was dubbed the green revolution. Yet with world population spiraling toward nine billion by mid-century, these experts now say we need a repeat performance, doubling current food production by 2030.

In other words, we need another green revolution. And we need it in half the time.

Ever since our ancestors gave up hunting and gathering for plowing and planting some 12,000 years ago, our numbers have marched in lockstep with our agricultural prowess. Each advance—the domestication of animals, irrigation, wet rice production—led to a corresponding jump in human population. Every time food supplies plateaued, population eventually leveled off. Early Arab and Chinese writers noted the relationship between population and food resources, but it wasn't until the end of the 18th century that a British scholar tried to explain the exact mechanism linking the two—and became perhaps the most vilified social scientist in history.

Thomas Robert Malthus, the namesake of such terms as "Malthusian collapse" and "Malthusian curse," was a mild-mannered mathematician, a

> The power of population is **indefinitely greater** than the power in the earth to produce substance for man.

clergyman—and, his critics would say, the ultimate glass-half-empty kind of guy. When a few Enlightenment philosophers, giddy from the success of the French Revolution, began predicting the continued unfettered improvement of the human condition, Malthus cut them off at the knees. Human population, he observed, increases at a geometric rate, doubling about every 25 years if unchecked, while agricultural production increases arithmetically—much more slowly. Therein lay a biological trap that humanity could never escape.

"The power of population is indefinitely greater than the power in the earth to produce subsistence for man," he wrote in his *Essay on the Principle of Population* in 1798. "This implies a strong and constantly operating check on population from the difficulty of subsistence." Malthus thought such checks could be voluntary, such as birth control, abstinence, or delayed marriage—or involuntary, through the scourges of war, famine, and disease. He advocated against food relief for all but the poorest of people, since he felt such aid encouraged more children to be born into misery. That tough love earned him a nasty cameo in English literature from none other than Charles Dickens. When Ebenezer Scrooge is asked to give alms for the poor in *A Christmas Carol*, the heartless banker tells the do-gooders that the destitute should head for the workhouses or prisons. And if they'd rather die than go there, "they had better do it, and decrease the surplus population."

The industrial revolution and plowing up of the English commons dramatically increased the amount of food in England, sweeping Malthus into the dustbin of the Victorian era. But it was the green revolution that truly made the reverend the laughingstock of modern economists. From 1950 to today the world has experienced the largest population growth in human history. After Malthus's time, six billion people were added to the planet's dinner tables. Yet thanks to improved methods of grain production, most of those people were fed. We'd finally shed Malthusian limits for good.

Or so we thought.

Even with the global recession, times are still relatively good in the southeastern province of Guangdong, where Yaotian sits tucked between postage-stamp garden plots and block after block of new factories that helped make the province one of the most prosperous in China. When times are good, the Chinese eat pigs. Lots of pigs. Per capita pork consumption in the world's most populous country went up 45 percent between 1993 and 2005, from 53 to 77 pounds a year.

That's good news for the average pork-loving Chinese—who still eats only about 40 percent as much meat as consumers in the United States. But it's worrisome for the world's grain supplies. It's no coincidence that as countries like China and India prosper and their people move up the food ladder, demand for grain has increased. For as tasty as that sweet-and-sour pork may be, eating meat is an incredibly inefficient way to feed oneself. It takes up to five times more grain to get the equivalent amount of calories from eating pork as from simply eating grain itself—ten times if we're talking about grain-fattened U.S. beef. As more grain has been diverted to livestock and to the production of biofuels for cars, annual worldwide consumption of grain has risen from 815 million metric tons in 1960 to 2.16 billion in 2008. Since 2005, the mad rush to biofuels alone has pushed grain-consumption growth from about 20 million tons annually to 50 million tons, according to Lester Brown of the Earth Policy Institute.

Even China, the second largest corn-growing nation on the planet, can't grow enough grain to feed all its pigs. Most of the shortfall is made up with imported soybeans from the United States or Brazil, one of the few countries with the potential to expand its cropland—often by plowing up rain forest. Increasing demand for food, feed, and biofuels has been a major driver of deforestation in the tropics. Between 1980 and 2000 more than half of new cropland acreage in the tropics was carved out of intact rain forests; Brazil alone increased its soybean acreage in Amazonia 10 percent a year from 1990 to 2005.

Some of those Brazilian soybeans may end up in the troughs of Guangzhou Lizhi Farms, the largest CAFO in Guangdong Province. Tucked into a green valley just off a four-lane highway that's still being built, some 60 white hog houses are scattered around large ponds, part of the waste-treatment system for 100,000 hogs. The city of Guangzhou is also building a brand-new meatpacking plant that will slaughter 5,000 head a day. By the time China has 1.5 billion people, sometime in the next 20 years, some experts predict they'll need another 200 million hogs just to keep up. And that's just China. World meat consumption is expected to double by 2050. That means we're going to need a whole lot more grain.

This isn't the first time the world has stood at the brink of a food crisis—it's only the most recent iteration. At 83, Gurcharan Singh Kalkat has lived long enough to remember one of the worst famines of the 20th century. In 1943 as many as four million people died in the "Malthusian correction" known as the Bengal Famine. For the following two decades, India had to import millions of tons of grain to feed its people. Then came the green revolution. In the mid-1960s, as India was struggling to feed its people during yet another crippling drought, a U.S. plant breeder named Norman Borlaug was working with Indian researchers to bring his high-yielding wheat varieties to Punjab. The new seeds were a godsend, says Kalkat, who was deputy director of agriculture for Punjab at the time. By 1970, farmers had nearly tripled their production with the same amount of work. "We had a big problem with what to do with the surplus," says Kalkat. "We closed schools one month early to store the wheat crop in the buildings."

Borlaug was born in Iowa and saw his mission as spreading the high-yield farming methods that had turned the American Midwest into the world's breadbasket to impoverished places throughout the world. His new dwarf wheat varieties, with their short, stocky stems supporting full, fat seed heads, were a startling breakthrough. They could produce grain like no other wheat ever seen—as long as there was plenty of water and synthetic fertilizer and little competition from weeds or insects.

To that end, the Indian government subsidized canals, fertilizer, and the drilling of tube wells for irrigation and gave farmers free electricity to pump the water. The new wheat varieties quickly spread throughout Asia, changing the traditional farming practices of millions of farmers, and were soon followed by new strains of "miracle" rice. The new crops matured faster and enabled farmers to grow two crops a year instead of one. Today a double crop of wheat, rice, or cotton is the norm in Punjab, which, with neighboring Haryana, recently supplied more than 90 percent of the wheat needed by grain-deficient states in India.

The green revolution Borlaug started had nothing to do with the eco-friendly green label in vogue today. With its use of synthetic fertilizers and pesticides to nurture vast fields of the same crop, a practice known as monoculture, this new method of industrial farming was the antithesis of today's organic trend. Rather, William S. Gaud, then administrator of the U.S. Agency for International Development, coined the phrase in 1968 to describe an alternative to Russia's red revolution, in which workers, soldiers, and hungry peasants had rebelled violently against the tsarist government. The more pacifying green revolution was such a staggering success that Borlaug won the Nobel Peace Prize in 1970.

Today, though, the miracle of the green revolution is over in Punjab: Yield growth has essentially flattened since the mid-1990s. Over-irrigation has led to steep drops in the water table, now tapped by 1.3 million tube wells, while thousands of hectares of productive land have been lost to salinization and waterlogged soils. Forty years of intensive irrigation, fertilization, and pesticides have not been kind to the loamy gray fields of Punjab. Nor, in some cases, to the people themselves.

In the dusty farming village of Bhuttiwala, home to some 6,000 people in the Muktsar district, village elder Jagsir Singh, in flowing beard and cobalt turban, adds up the toll: "We've had

We're now poised to see probably the greatest period of fundamental scientific advance in the history of agriculture.

49 deaths due to cancer in the last four years," he says. "Most of them were young people. The water is not good. It's poisonous, contaminated water. Yet people still drink it."

Walking through the narrow dirt lanes past pyramids of dried cow dung, Singh introduces Amarjeet Kaur, a slender 40-year-old who for years drew the family's daily water from a hand pump in their brick-hard compound. She was diagnosed with breast cancer last year. Tej Kaur, 50, also has breast cancer. Her surgery, she says, wasn't nearly as painful as losing her seven-year-old grandson to "blood cancer," or leukemia. Jagdev Singh is a sweet-faced 14-year-old boy whose spine is slowly deteriorating. From his wheelchair, he is watching *SpongeBob SquarePants* dubbed in Hindi as his father discusses his prognosis. "The doctors say he will not live to see 20," says Bhola Singh.

There's no proof these cancers were caused by pesticides. But researchers have found pesticides in the Punjabi farmers' blood, their water table, their vegetables, even their wives' breast milk. So many people take the train from the Malwa region to the cancer hospital in Bikaner that it's now called the Cancer Express. The government is concerned enough to spend millions on reverse-osmosis water-treatment plants for the worst affected villages.

If that weren't worrisome enough, the high cost of fertilizers and pesticides has plunged many Punjabi farmers into debt. One study found more than 1,400 cases of farmer suicides in 93 villages between 1988 and 2006. Some groups put the total for the state as high as 40,000 to 60,000 suicides over that period. Many drank pesticides or hung themselves in their fields.

"The green revolution has brought us only downfall," says Jarnail Singh, a retired schoolteacher in Jajjal village. "It ruined our soil, our environment, our water table. Used to be we had fairs in villages where people would come together and have fun. Now we gather in medical centers. The government has sacrificed the people of Punjab for grain."

Others, of course, see it differently. Rattan Lal, a noted soil scientist at Ohio State who graduated from Punjab Agricultural University in 1963, believes it was the abuse—not the use—of green revolution technologies that caused most of the problems. That includes the overuse of fertilizers, pesticides, and irrigation and the removal of all crop residues from the fields, essentially strip-mining soil nutrients. "I realize the problems of water quality and water withdrawal," says Lal. "But it saved hundreds of millions of people. We paid a price in water, but the choice was to let people die."

In terms of production, the benefits of the green revolution are hard to deny. India hasn't experienced famine since Borlaug brought his seeds to town, while world grain production has more than doubled. Some scientists credit increased rice yields alone with the existence of 700 million more people on the planet.

Many crop scientists and farmers believe the solution to our current food crisis lies in a second green revolution, based largely on our newfound knowledge of the gene. Plant breeders now know the sequence of nearly all of the 50,000 or so genes in corn and soybean plants and are using that knowledge in ways that were unimaginable only four or five years ago, says Robert Fraley, chief technology officer for the agricultural giant Monsanto. Fraley is convinced that genetic modification, which allows breeders to bolster crops with beneficial traits from other species, will lead to new varieties with higher yields, reduced fertilizer needs, and drought tolerance—the holy grail for the past decade. He believes biotech will make it possible to double yields of Monsanto's core crops of corn, cotton, and soybeans by 2030. "We're now poised to see probably the greatest period of fundamental scientific advance in the history of agriculture."

Africa is the continent where *Homo sapiens* was born, and with its worn-out soils, fitful rain, and rising population, it could very well offer a glimpse of our species' future. For numerous reasons—lack of infrastructure, corruption, inaccessible markets—the green revolution never made it here. Agricultural production per capita actually declined in sub-Saharan Africa between 1970 and 2000, while the population soared, leaving an average ten-million-ton annual food deficit. It's now home to more than a quarter of the world's hungriest people.

Tiny, landlocked Malawi, dubbed the "warm heart of Africa" by a hopeful tourism industry, is also in the hungry heart of Africa, a poster child for the continent's agricultural ills. Living in one of the poorest and most densely populated countries in Africa, the majority of Malawians are corn farmers who eke out a living on less than two dollars a day. In 2005 the rains failed once again in Malawi, and more than a third of its population of 13 million required food aid to survive. Malawi's President Bingu wa Mutharika declared he did not get elected to rule a nation of beggars. After initially failing to persuade the World Bank and other donors to help subsidize green revolution inputs, Bingu, as he's known here, decided to spend $58 million from the country's own coffers to get hybrid seeds and fertilizers into the hands of poor farmers. The World Bank eventually got on board and persuaded Bingu to target the subsidy to the poorest farmers. About 1.3 million farm families received coupons that allowed them to buy three kilograms of hybrid corn seed and two 50-kilogram bags of fertilizer at a third of the market price.

What happened next has been called the Malawi Miracle. Good seed and a little fertilizer—and the return of soil-soaking rains—helped farmers reap bumper crops for the next two years. (Last year's harvests, however, were slightly down.) The 2007 harvest was estimated to be 3.44 million metric tons, a national record. "They went from a 44 percent deficit to an 18 percent surplus, doubling their production," says Pedro Sanchez, the director of the Tropical Agriculture Program at Columbia University who advised the Malawi government on the program. "The next year they had a 53 percent surplus and exported maize to Zimbabwe. It was a dramatic change."

So dramatic, in fact, that it has led to an increasing awareness of the importance of agricultural investment in *(Continued on page 84)*

ETHIOPIA

The sorghum porridge at this refugee camp lacks the protein and fat needed for an Afari mother to produce enough milk to breast-feed her malnourished son. Thousands of pastoral Afaris have fled here from nearby Eritrea to escape war and drought. The green revolution that brought high-yield grain to Asia in the 1960s never reached sub-Saharan Africa, where crop production per capita has declined in recent decades.

(*Continued from page 81*) reducing poverty and hunger in places like Malawi. In October 2007 the World Bank issued a critical report, concluding that the agency, international donors, and African governments had fallen short in helping Africa's poor farmers and had neglected investment in agriculture for the previous 15 years. After decades of discouraging public investment in agriculture and calling for market-based solutions that rarely materialized, institutions like the World Bank have reversed course and pumped funds into agriculture over the past two years.

Malawi's subsidy program is part of a larger movement to bring the green revolution, at long last, to Africa. Since 2006 the Rockefeller Foundation and the Bill and Melinda Gates Foundation have ponied up nearly half a billion dollars to fund the Alliance for a Green Revolution in Africa, focused primarily on bringing plant-breeding programs to African universities and enough fertilizer to farmers' fields. Columbia's Sanchez, along with über-economist and poverty warrior Jeffrey Sachs, is providing concrete examples of the benefits of such investment in 80 small villages clustered into about a dozen "Millennium Villages" scattered in hunger hot spots throughout Africa. With the help of a few rock stars and A-list actors, Sanchez and Sachs are spending $300,000 a year on each small village. That's one-third as much per person as Malawi's per capita GDP, leading many in the development community to wonder if such a program can be sustained over the long haul.

But is a reprise of the green revolution—with the traditional package of synthetic fertilizers, pesticides, and irrigation, supercharged by genetically engineered seeds—really the answer to the world's food crisis? Last year a massive study called the "International Assessment of Agricultural Knowledge, Science and Technology for Development" concluded that the immense production increases brought about by science and technology in the past 30 years have failed to improve food access for many of the world's poor. The six-year study, initiated by the World Bank and the UN's Food and Agriculture Organization and involving some 400 agricultural experts from around the globe, called for a paradigm shift in agriculture toward more sustainable and ecologically friendly practices that would benefit the world's 900 million small farmers, not just agribusiness.

The green revolution's legacy of tainted soil and depleted aquifers is one reason to look for new strategies. So is what author and University of California, Berkeley, professor Michael Pollan calls the Achilles heel of current green revolution methods: a dependence on fossil fuels. Natural gas, for example, is a raw material for nitrogen fertilizers. "The only way you can have one farmer feed 140 Americans is with monocultures. And monocultures need lots of fossil-fuel-based fertilizers and lots of fossil-fuel-based pesticides," Pollan says. "That only works in an era of cheap fossil fuels, and that era is coming to an end. Moving anyone to a dependence on fossil fuels seems the height of irresponsibility."

So far, genetic breakthroughs that would free green revolution crops from their heavy dependence on irrigation and fertilizer have proved elusive. Engineering plants that can fix their own nitrogen or are resistant to drought "has proven a lot harder than they thought," says Pollan. Monsanto's Fraley predicts his company will have drought-tolerant corn in the U.S. market by 2012. But the increased yields promised during drought years are only 6 to 10 percent above those of standard drought-hammered crops.

And so a shift has already begun to small, underfunded projects scattered across Africa and Asia. Some call it agroecology, others sustainable agriculture, but the underlying idea is revolutionary: that we must stop focusing on simply maximizing grain yields at any cost and consider the environmental and social impacts of food production. Vandana Shiva is a nuclear physicist turned agroecologist who is India's harshest critic of the green revolution. "I call it monocultures of the mind," she says. "They just look at yields of wheat and rice, but overall the food basket is going down. There were 250 kinds of crops in Punjab before the green revolution." Shiva argues that small-scale, biologically diverse farms can produce more food with fewer petroleum-based inputs. Her research has shown that using compost instead of natural-gas-derived fertilizer increases organic matter in the soil, sequestering carbon and holding moisture—two key advantages for farmers facing climate change. "If you are talking about solving the food crisis, these are the methods you need," adds Shiva.

In northern Malawi one project is getting many of the same results as the Millennium Villages project, at a fraction of the cost. There are no hybrid corn seeds, free fertilizers, or new roads here in the village of Ekwendeni. Instead the Soils, Food and Healthy Communities (SFHC) project distributes legume seeds, recipes, and technical advice for growing nutritious crops like peanuts, pigeon peas, and soybeans, which enrich the soil by fixing nitrogen while also enriching children's diets. The program began in 2000 at Ekwendeni Hospital, where the staff was seeing high rates of malnutrition. Research suggested the culprit was the corn monoculture that had left small farmers with poor yields due to depleted soils and the high price of fertilizer.

The project's old pickup needs a push to get it going, but soon Boyd Zimba, the project's assistant coordinator, and Zacharia Nkhonya, its food-security supervisor, are rattling down the road, talking about what they see as the downside of the Malawi Miracle. "First, the fertilizer subsidy cannot last long," says Nkhonya, a compact man with a quick smile. "Second, it doesn't go to everyone. And third, it only comes once a year, while legumes are long-term—soils get improved every year, unlike with fertilizers."

At the small village of Encongolweni, a group of two dozen SFHC farmers greet us with a song about the dishes they make from soybeans and pigeon peas. We sit in their meetinghouse as if at an old-time tent revival, as they testify about how planting legumes has changed their lives. Ackim Mhone's story is typical. By incorporating legumes into his rotation, he's doubled his corn yield on his small plot of land while cutting his fertilizer use in half. "That was enough to change the life of my family," Mhone says, and to enable him to improve his house and buy livestock. Later, Alice Sumphi, a 67-year-old farmer with a mischievous smile, dances in her plot of young knee-high tomatoes, proudly pointing out that they bested those of the younger men. Canadian

researchers found that after eight years, the children of more than 7,000 families involved in the project showed significant weight increases, making a pretty good case that soil health and community health are connected in Malawi.

Which is why the project's research coordinator, Rachel Bezner Kerr, is alarmed that big-money foundations are pushing for a new green revolution in Africa. "I find it deeply disturbing," she says. "It's getting farmers to rely on expensive inputs produced from afar that are making money for big companies rather than on agro-ecological methods for using local resources and skills. I don't think that's the solution."

Regardless of which model prevails—agriculture as a diverse ecological art, as a high-tech industry, or some combination of the two—the challenge of putting enough food in nine billion mouths by 2050 is daunting. Two billion people already live in the driest parts of the globe, and climate change is projected to slash yields in these regions even further. No matter how great their yield potential, plants still need water to grow. And in the not too distant future, every year could be a drought year for much of the globe.

New climate studies show that extreme heat waves, such as the one that withered crops and killed thousands in western Europe in 2003, are very likely to become common in the tropics and subtropics by century's end. Himalayan glaciers that now provide water for hundreds of millions of people, livestock, and farmland in China and India are melting faster and could vanish completely by 2035. In the worst-case scenario, yields for some grains could decline by 10 to 15 percent in South Asia by 2030. Projections for southern Africa are even more dire. In a region already racked by water scarcity and food insecurity, the all-important corn harvest could drop by 30 percent—47 percent in the worst-case scenario. All the while the population clock keeps ticking, with a net of 2.5 more mouths to feed born every second. That amounts to 4,500 more mouths in the time it takes you to read this article.

Which leads us, inevitably, back to Malthus.

On a brisk fall day that has put color into the cheeks of the most die-hard Londoners, I visit the British Library and check out the first edition of the book that still generates such heated debate. Malthus's *Essay on the Principle of Population* looks like an eighth-grade science primer. From its strong, clear prose comes the voice of a humble parish priest who hoped, as much as anything, to be proved wrong.

"People who say Malthus is wrong usually haven't read him," says Tim Dyson, a professor of population studies at the London School of Economics. "He was not taking a view any different than what Adam Smith took in the first volume of *The Wealth of Nations.* No one in their right mind doubts the idea that populations have to live within their resource base. And that the capacity of society to increase resources from that base is ultimately limited."

Though his essays emphasized "positive checks" on population from famine, disease, and war, his "preventative checks" may have been more important. A growing workforce, Malthus explained, depresses wages, which tends to make people delay marriage until they can better support a family. Delaying marriage reduces fertility rates, creating an equally powerful check on populations. It has now been shown that this is the basic mechanism that regulated population growth in western Europe for some 300 years before the industrial revolution—a pretty good record for *any* social scientist, says Dyson.

Yet when Britain recently issued a new 20-pound note, it put Adam Smith on the back, not T. R. Malthus. He doesn't fit the ethos of the moment. We don't want to think about limits. But as we approach nine billion people on the planet, all clamoring for the same opportunities, the same lifestyles, the same hamburgers, we ignore them at our risk.

None of the great classical economists saw the industrial revolution coming, or the transformation of economies and agriculture that it would bring about. The cheap, readily available energy contained in coal—and later in other fossil fuels—unleashed the greatest increase in food, personal wealth, and people the world has ever seen, enabling Earth's population to increase sevenfold since Malthus's day. And yet hunger, famine, and malnutrition are with us still, just as Malthus said they would be.

"Years ago I was working with a Chinese demographer," Dyson says. "One day he pointed out to me the two Chinese characters above his office door that spelled the word 'population.' You had the character for a person and the character for an open mouth. It really struck me. Ultimately there has to be a balance between population and resources. And this notion that we can continue to grow forever, well it's ridiculous."

Perhaps somewhere deep in his crypt in Bath Abbey, Malthus is quietly wagging a bony finger and saying, "Told you so."

Discussion Questions

- In what ways might the term "green revolution," used to refer to the Indian programs initiated in the 1960s, seem misleading when viewed from today's perspective?

- What price did Indian communities pay for the change in agricultural methods that had helped combat famine 50 years ago? Was that price worth the benefits achieved?

- What role does crop science play in providing better yields for developing countries, and what are the hidden costs of using biotechnology?

- How have new concepts of sustainable agriculture challenged or replaced assumptions about traditional methods used to create the first green revolution?

Writing Activities

- Write an essay in which you evaluate the possible trade-offs of preventing widespread famine using potentially dangerous pesticides and/or bio-engineered seeds that may carry significant or unknown health risks. After examining the pros and cons, which side, in your view, comes out on top? Explain.

- Do you support the use of bio-engineered products like drought- or pest-resistant seeds to enhance food production in famine-threatened countries? Why or why not? Be persuasive by citing facts accurately, presenting effective examples, and including a carefully constructed counterargument.

- State the challenges that make "putting enough food in nine billion mouths by 2050" such a difficult problem to solve. Do you think the world is prepared to meet these challenges? Following your explanation of the problem, present a well-reasoned argument to support your view about whether or not we have the knowledge, the resources, and the will to solve it.

- Building from his conversation with British professor Tim Dyson, the author states, "while we don't want to think about limits... as we approach nine billion people on the planet, all clamoring for the same opportunities, the same lifestyles, the same hamburgers, we ignore them at our risk" (86). Write an essay that begins by paraphrasing Bourne's statement and explaining what you think he means. Then present a detailed vision of what the world might look like 50 years from now if we continue to ignore the limits to which he refers or, alternatively, if we take measures to address them. Be as specific as possible.

Collaborative Activities

- What are the risks the world faces if changes are not made in methods of food production around the world? Working together, list the specific problems that need to be solved, and discuss among your group members whether or not these can be successfully addressed with technology or other methods currently available. Present your group's conclusions to the class.

- Working in a small group, examine the role richer nations play in helping to prevent a global food crisis. Discuss the relationship between wealthier nations and poorer ones as it relates to food production, technology, climate, and natural resources, and identify the key elements. Assign responsible parties to each element.

STILL WATERS: THE GLOBAL FISH CRISIS

Life in the world's oceans may only come into our daily lives in the form of a sandwich or a sushi dinner. "Still Waters: The Global Fish Crisis" examines how technologically fortified overfishing in once abundant waters has brought a most profitable and highly desired fish, also an important link in the ocean's food chain, to the brink of population collapse.

As you read "Still Waters: The Global Fish Crisis," consider the following questions:

- How have recent changes in fishing methods have enhanced profitability and facilitated depletion of tuna populations?
- What is the role demand plays in large-scale fishing practices?
- What are the long-term consequences of poorly regulated and illegal fishing practices?
- What is the role international regulations may play in restoring ocean fish populations?

To supply the world's sushi markets, the magnificent giant bluefin tuna is fished in the Mediterranean at four times the sustainable rate. These bluefin are being fattened off Spain at one of 69 ranches that have sprung up in the Mediterranean in the past decade, demolishing stocks of the fish.

STILL WATERS:
THE GLOBAL
FISH CRISIS

With competition intensifying to supply mostly European markets, fishing grounds off West Africa are going the way of Europe's: toward depletion. These Senegalese, who had hoped to catch desirable export species such as shrimp or sole, will *throw away the fish in their nets* — wasting valuable protein for Africa.

FISHERMAN SEE DOLLAR SIGNS. WE SEE
THE WORLD'S MOST MAGNIFICENT FISH BECOMING EXTINCT
RIGHT BEFORE OUR EYES. IS IT TOO LATE TO SAVE THEM?

> **The world's oceans are a shadow of what they once were.**

No more magnificent fish swims the world's oceans than the giant bluefin tuna, which can grow to 12 feet in length, weigh 1,500 pounds, and live for 30 years. Despite its size, it is an exquisitely hydrodynamic creation, able to streak through water at 25 miles an hour and dive deeper than half a mile. Unlike most other fish, it has a warm-blooded circulatory system that enables it to roam from the Arctic to the tropics. Once, giant bluefin migrated by the millions throughout the Atlantic Basin and the Mediterranean Sea, their flesh so important to the people of the ancient world that they painted the tuna's likeness on cave walls and minted its image on coins.

The giant, or Atlantic, bluefin possesses another extraordinary attribute, one that may prove to be its undoing: Its buttery belly meat, liberally layered with fat, is considered the finest sushi in the world. Over the past decade, a high-tech armada, often guided by spotter planes, has pursued giant bluefin from one end of the Mediterranean to the other, annually netting tens of thousands of the fish, many of them illegally. The bluefin are fattened offshore in sea cages before being shot and butchered for the sushi and steak markets in Japan, America, and Europe. So many giant bluefin have been hauled out of the Mediterranean that the population is in danger of collapse. Meanwhile, European and North African officials have done little to stop the slaughter.

"My big fear is that it may be too late," said Sergi Tudela, a Spanish marine biologist with the World Wildlife Fund, which has led the struggle to rein in the bluefin fishery. "I have a very graphic image in my mind. It is of the migration of so many buffalo in the American West in the early 19th century. It was the same with bluefin tuna in the Mediterranean, a migration of a massive number of animals. And now we are witnessing the same phenomenon happening to giant bluefin tuna that we saw happen with America's buffalo. We are witnessing this, right now, right before our eyes."

Adapted from "Still Waters: The Global Fish Crisis"
by Fen Montaigne: National Geographic Magazine,
April 2007.

The decimation of giant bluefin is emblematic of everything wrong with global fisheries today: the vastly increased killing power of new fishing technology, the shadowy network of international companies making huge profits from the trade, negligent fisheries management and enforcement, and consumers' indifference to the fate of the fish they choose to buy.

The world's oceans are a shadow of what they once were. With a few notable exceptions, such as well-managed fisheries in Alaska, Iceland, and New Zealand, the number of fish swimming the seas is a fraction of what it was a century ago. Marine biologists differ on the extent of the decline. Some argue that stocks of many large oceangoing fish have fallen by 80 to 90 percent, while others say the declines have been less steep. But all agree that, in most places, too many boats are chasing too few fish.

Popular species such as cod have plummeted from the North Sea to Georges Bank off New England. In the Mediterranean, 12 species of shark are commercially extinct, and swordfish there, which should grow as thick as a telephone pole, are now caught as juveniles and eaten when no bigger than a baseball bat. With many Northern Hemisphere waters fished out, commercial fleets have steamed south, overexploiting once teeming fishing grounds. Off West Africa, poorly regulated fleets, both local and foreign, are wiping out fish stocks from the productive waters of the continental shelf, depriving subsistence fishermen in Senegal, Ghana, Guinea, Angola, and other countries of their families' main source of protein. In Asia, so many boats have fished the waters of the Gulf of Thailand and the Java Sea that stocks are close to exhaustion. "The oceans are suffering from a lot of things, but the one that

> The oceans are suffering from a lot of things, but **the one that overshadows everything else** is fishing.

overshadows everything else is fishing," said Joshua S. Reichert of the Pew Charitable Trusts. "And unless we get a handle on the extraction of fish and marine resources, we will lose much of the life that remains in the sea."

"Cruel" may seem a harsh indictment of the age-old profession of fishing—and certainly does not apply to all who practice the trade—but how else to portray the world's shark fishermen, who kill tens of millions of sharks a year, large numbers finned alive for shark-fin soup and allowed to sink to the bottom to die? How else to characterize the incalculable number of fish and other sea creatures scooped up in nets, allowed to suffocate, and dumped overboard as useless by-catch? Or the longline fisheries, whose miles and miles of baited hooks attract—and drown—creatures such as the loggerhead turtle and wandering albatross?

Do we countenance such loss because fish live in a world we cannot see? Would it be different if, as one conservationist fantasized, the fish wailed as we lifted them out of the water in nets? If the giant bluefin lived on land, its size, speed, and epic migrations would ensure its legendary status, with tourists flocking to photograph it in national parks. But because it lives in the sea, its majesty—comparable to that of a lion—lies largely beyond comprehension.

One of the ironies—and tragedies—of the Mediterranean bluefin hunt is that the very act of procreation now puts the fish at the mercy of the fleets. In the spring and summer, as the water warms, schools of bluefin rise to the surface to spawn. Slashing through the sea, planing on their sides and exposing their massive silver-colored flanks, the large females each expel tens of millions of eggs, and the males emit clouds of milt. From the air, on a calm day, this turmoil of reproduction—the flashing of fish, the disturbed sea, the slick of spawn and sperm—can be seen from miles away by spotter planes, which call in the fleet.

On a warm July morning, in the sapphire-colored waters west of the Spanish island of Ibiza, six purse-seine boats from three competing companies searched for giant bluefin tuna. The purse seiners—named for their conical, purse-like nets, which are drawn closed from the bottom—were guided by three spotter aircraft that crisscrossed the sky like vultures.

In the center of the action was Txema Galaz Ugalde, a Basque marine biologist, diver, and fisherman who helps run Ecolofish, one of 69 tuna ranching, or fattening, operations that have sprung up throughout the Mediterranean. A small company, Ecolofish owns five purse seiners. Its main rival that morning was the tuna baron of the Mediterranean, Francisco Fuentes of Ricardo Fuentes & Sons, whose industrial-scale operations have been chewing up giant bluefin stocks.

I was with Galaz on *La Viveta Segunda*—a 72-foot support vessel that was part of the fleet of dive boats and cage-towing tugs following the purse seiners. Around 11 a.m., the spotter planes spied a school, setting the purse seiners on a 19-knot dash. The stakes were high. Even a small school of 200 bluefin can, when fattened, fetch more than half a million dollars on the Japanese market, Galaz watched through binoculars as an Ecolofish seiner reached the school first and began encircling it with a mile-long net.

"He's fishing!" Galaz shouted. "He's shooting the net!"

It was not an unalloyed victory. Before Ecolofish's boat could complete its circle, a Fuentes seiner rushed forward and stopped just short of the unfurling net. Under one of the few rules that exist in the free-for-all for Mediterranean bluefin, this symbolic touch entitled the competing boat to split the catch fifty-fifty.

Over the next several hours, Galaz and his divers transferred the fish—163 bluefin, averaging about 300 pounds—from the purse-seine net into the sea cage, a large holding pen about 160 feet in diameter, with a sturdy plastic frame supporting a heavy mesh net. As the pen, already brimming with a thousand bluefin caught in the days before, was aligned with the purse-seine net, Galaz invited me into the water.

Swimming with the tuna was mesmerizing but unsettling. Giant bluefin are, as Galaz put it, "like missiles, prepared for speed and power." Their backs were battleship gray topped with a saw-toothed line of small yellow dorsal fins. Their sides had the look of battered chrome and steel; some bore the streak of an electric blue line. The larger fish, weighing more than 500 pounds, were at least eight feet long.

Ecolofish's catch was part of an annual legal take of 32,000 tons in the Mediterranean and eastern Atlantic, The true quantity, however, is closer to between 50,000 and 60,000 tons. The group charged with managing bluefin tuna stocks, the International Commission for the Conservation of Atlantic Tuna (ICCAT), has acknowledged that the fleet has been violating quotas egregiously. Scientists estimate that if fishing continues at

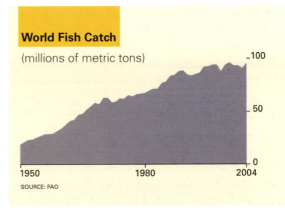

World Fish Catch

(millions of metric tons)

SOURCE: FAO

current levels, stocks are bound to collapse. But despite strong warnings from its own biologists, ICCAT—with 43 member states—refused to reduce quotas significantly last November, over the objections of delegations from the United States, Canada, and a handful of other nations. Because bluefin sometimes migrate across the Atlantic, American scientists, and bluefin fishermen who abide by small quotas off their coasts, have long been calling for a large reduction in the Mediterranean catch.

"The Mediterranean is at the point that if bluefin stocks are not actually collapsing, they are approaching collapse," said William T. Hogarth, ICCAT's recently appointed chairman, who also serves as director of the U.S. National Marine Fisheries Service, "I was really disappointed—when it got to bluefin, science just seemed to go out the window. The bottom line was that, as chairman, I felt I was sort of presiding over the demise of one of fire most magnificent fish that swims the ocean."

The story of giant bluefin tuna began with unfathomable abundance, as they surged through the Straits of Gibraltar each spring, fanning out across the Mediterranean to spawn. Over millennia, fishermen devised a method of extending nets from shore to intercept the fish and funnel them into chambers, where they were slaughtered. By the mid-1800s, a hundred tuna traps—known as *tonnara* in Italy and *almadraba* in Spain—harvested up to 15,000 tons of bluefin annually. The fishery was sustainable, supporting thousands of workers and their families.

Today, all but a dozen or so of the trap fisheries have closed, primarily for lack of fish but also because of coastal development

Large females, capable of producing 40 million eggs, are being wiped out.

and pollution. One of the few that remains is the renowned tonnara, founded by Arabs in the ninth century, on the island of Favignana off Sicily. In 1864, Favignana's fishermen took a record 14,020 bluefin, averaging 425 pounds, Last year, so few fish were caught—about 100, averaging 65 pounds—that Favignana held only one *mattanza*, which occurs when the tuna, are channeled into a netted chamber and lifted to the surface by fishermen who kill them with gaffs. One sign of the Favignana tonnara's diminishment is that it is run by a Rome marketing executive, Chiara Zarlocco, whose plan for the future is to dress the fishermen in historic costumes as they reenact the mattanza.

The big trouble for Atlantic bluefin began in the mid-1990s. By then, stocks of southern bluefin tuna—which, along with Pacific bluefin and Atlantic bluefin, compose the world's three bluefin species, all treasured for sushi—had been fished to between 6 and 12 percent of the original numbers in the South Pacific and Indian Oceans. As the Japanese searched for new sources, they turned to the Mediterranean, where bluefin reserves were still large.

In 1996, Croatians who had developed techniques for fattening southern bluefin in Australia established the first Mediterranean tuna ranch, in the Adriatic. The process is simple. Newly caught bluefin are transferred to coastal sea cages, where—for months, even years—they are fed oily fish such as anchovies or sardines to give their flesh the high fat content so prized in Japan.

The prospect of producing a steady—and highly profitable—supply of fatly Mediterranean bluefin set off a cascade of events that has proved disastrous. The Mediterranean fleet has increased its fishing effort threefold, with the bluefin flotilla now totaling 1,700 vessels, including 314 purse seiners. Compounding the problem, the advent of tuna ranching made it difficult for the European Union and national governments to enforce quotas. Bluefin are netted at sea, transferred into cages at sea, fattened offshore, killed offshore, and flash-frozen on Japanese ships. As Masanori Miyahara of the Fisheries Agency of Japan, and a former ICCAT chairman, told me: "It's kind of a black box."

The spread of tuna ranching means that bluefin are being wiped out at all stages of their life cycle. In Croatia, for instance, the industry is based almost entirely on fattening juveniles for two to three years, which means fish are killed before they spawn. Elsewhere, in places such as the Balearic Islands, large females, capable of producing 40 million eggs, are being wiped out. In just ten years, bluefin populations have been driven down sharply.

"What's happening is a bit like what happened to cod," said Jean-Marc Fromentin, a marine biologist and bluefin expert with IFREMER, the French Research Institute for the Exploitation of the Sea. "You don't see the decrease right away because you have had a huge accumulation of biomass. But it's like having a bank account, and you keep taking much more out than you're putting in."

At the heart of the fishing activity is Francisco Fuentes and his Cartagena-based company, Ricardo Fuentes & Sons, which, according to industry experts, controls 60 percent of the giant bluefin ranching business in the Mediterranean, generating revenues of more than 220 million dollars a year, according to industry sources. (A Fuentes spokesman said revenues are roughly half that.) In partnership with the Japanese giants Mitsui, Mitsubishi, and Maruha, the Fuentes Group—with the help of EU and Spanish subsidies—has bought the sea cages, tugs, and support boats needed for large-scale

fattening operations, Fuentes & Sons also formed partnerships with French and Spanish companies that owned 20 purse seiners—five-million-dollar vessels equipped with powerful sonar systems and nets that can encircle 3,000 adult bluefin.

With the Fuentes Group and its partners leading the way, the bluefin fleet methodically targeted the fish in the spawning grounds close to Europe, then turned its attention to untouched areas. The richest of these de facto reserves was Libya's Gulf of Sidra. "It was the tuna aquarium of the Mediterranean," recalled Roberto Mielgo Bregazzi, a tuna ranching consultant who first visited the Gulf of Sidra six years ago. "I've never seen anything like it. The average size of bluefin was 600 pounds. It was one of the last tuna Shangri-las,"

Mielgo Bregazzi, a dapper Spaniard and former professional diver who heads Advanced Tuna Ranching Technologies, has been on a mission to expose IUU—illegal, unreported, and unregulated—bluefin fishing. Drawing on a wide network of inside sources, as well as published information, he has written lengthy reports detailing the IUU bluefin business. Using arcane data such as the capacity and schedules of Japanese freezer vessels, he has shown that the Mediterranean tuna fleet has been seizing almost double its annual legal quota.

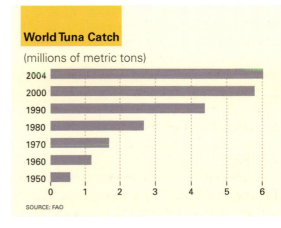

World Tuna Catch

(millions of metric tons)

SOURCE: FAO

Mielgo Bregazzi said Ricardo Fuentes & Sons and a French partner have worked with a Libyan company, Ras el Hillal, to catch giant bluefin in Libyan waters. Mielgo Bregazzi said that Seif al Islam Qaddafi, the son of Libyan leader Muammar Qaddafi, has a financial interest in Ras el Hillal and has earned millions of dollars from the bluefin fishery. Mielgo Bregazzi calculated that, for the past four years, bluefin fleets netted more than 10,000 tons of bluefin annually in Libyan waters. Some of the catch is legal under quotas for Libyan, Spanish, and French boats, but much of it appears to be caught illegally.

David Martinez Cañabate, assistant manager of the Fuentes Group, said the company has "absolutely" no connection to the Qaddafi family and that all bluefin tuna it catches, buys, or ranches have been legally caught and properly documented with ICCAT and Spanish authorities. He conceded that bluefin have been overfished, mainly by companies that do not ranch tuna but sell the fish soon after netting them. Fleets from other countries also catch bluefin without an ICCAT quota and ranch them

> They're slaughtering everything. **The fish don't stand a chance.**

illegally, Martinez said. He said much of Mielgo Bregazzi's information is "incorrect or, worse, bad intentioned" and that the Fuentes Group has supported stricter conservation measures. "We are more interested than anyone in the future of the tuna," Martinez said. "We live off this resource."

Actually, Libyan and other Mediterranean bluefin have so flooded the market that Japanese companies have stockpiled 20,000 tons in giant freezers. The glut has halved prices for fishermen in the past few years, to between three and four dollars a pound. Still, the value of the bluefin caught annually in Libya, then fattened for several months, is roughly 400 million dollars on the Japanese market.

"They're slaughtering everything," Mielgo Bregazzi said, "The fish don't stand a chance."

The extent to which giant bluefin fleets flout regulations became evident during a visit to the Italian island, of Lampedusa, south of Sicily. To give the tuna a reprieve during peak spawning season, EU and ICCAT rules prohibit spotter aircraft from flying in June. The regulation is often ignored.

I flew one June morning with Eduardo Domaniewicz, an Argentine-American pilot who has spotted tuna for French and Italian purse seiners since 2003. Riding shotgun was Domaniewicz's spotter, Alfonso Consiglio. They were combing the waters between Lampedusa and Tunisia, and they were not alone: Three other spotter aircraft were prowling illegally, relaying tuna sightings to some of the 20 purse seiners in the water below. (After two hours, high winds and choppy seas, which make it. difficult both to see and net the

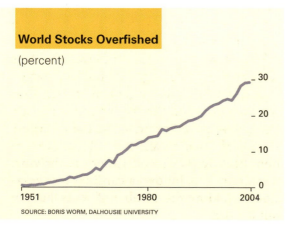

World Stocks Overfished

(percent)

SOURCE: BORIS WORM, DALHOUSIE UNIVERSITY

bluefin, forced the planes to return to Lampedusa and Malta.)

Domaniewicz was conflicted. He loved to fly and was well paid. He believed his June flights were legal, because Italy never agreed to the ban. But after three years of spotting for the bluefin fleet, he was fed up with the uncontrolled fishing. Just before I arrived on Lampedusa, he had watched two purse-seine fleets net 835,000 pounds of bluefin, sharing more than two million dollars.

"There is no way for the fish to escape—everything is high-tech," Domaniewicz said. Speaking of the French purse-seine fishermen he worked for in Libya, he said, "I am an environmentalist, and I couldn't stand the way they fished with no care for the quotas. I saw these people taking everything. They catch whatever they want. They just see money on the sea. They don't think what will be there in ten years."

Alfonso Consiglio, whose family owns a fleet of purse seiners, also is torn. "The price is cheap because more and more tuna are being caught," he said. "My only weapon is to catch more fish. It's a vicious circle. If I catch my quota of a thousand tuna, I can't live because the price is very cheap. I want to respect the quota, but I can't because I need to live. If boats of all countries respect the rules, tuna will not be finished. If only few countries respect the rules, and others don't respect the rules, the fisherman who respects rules is finished."

How can this endless cycle of overfishing be stopped? How can the world's fleets be prevented from committing ecological and economic suicide by depleting the oceans of bluefin tuna, shark, cod, haddock, sea buss, hake, red snapper, orange roughy, grouper, grenadier, sturgeon, plaice, rockfish, skate, and other species?

Experts agree that, first, the world's oceans must be managed as ecosystems, not simply as larders from which the fishing industry can extract protein at will. Second, the management councils that oversee fisheries, such as ICCAT, long dominated by commercial fishing interests, must share power with scientists and conservationists.

Further, governments must cut back the world's four million fishing vessels—nearly double what is needed to fish the ocean sustainably—and slash the estimated 25 billion dollars in government subsidies bestowed annually on the fishing industry.

In addition, fisheries agencies will have to set tough quotas and enforce them. For giant bluefin in the Mediterranean, that may mean shutting down the fishery during the spawning season and substantially increasing the minimum catch weight. ICCAT recently failed to decrease quotas significantly or close the fishery at peak spawn, although it did increase the minimum catch weight in most areas to 66 pounds and ban spotter aircraft. But without inspection and enforcement, the commission's new rules will, like the old ones, mean little.

Another crucial step, both in the Mediterranean and around the world, would be the creation of large marine protected areas. Also important are campaigns by such groups as the Marine Stewardship Council, which is working with consumers as well as retail giants to promote trade in sustainably caught fish.

The news from the fisheries front is not unremittingly grim. Indeed, where sound fisheries management exists, fish populations—and the fishing industry—are healthy. A prime example is Alaska, where stocks of Pacific salmon and pollock are bountiful. Iceland's cod fishery is thriving, because it, too, follows a cardinal conservation rule: Limit the number of boats that can pursue fish.

In a cascade of death, guitarfish, rays, and other by-catch are tossed from a shrimp boat in the Gulf of California. During the past decade, efforts to reduce by-catch have begun to pay off with better net and hook designs, pingers on nets to repel marine mammals, and streamers behind boats to frighten away seabirds.

© 2007 BRIAN J. SKERRY/National Geographic Stock

But all agree that the fundamental reform that must precede all others is not a change in regulations but a change in people's minds. The world must begin viewing the creatures that inhabit the sea much as it looks at wildlife on land. Only when fish are seen as wild things deserving of protection, only when the Mediterranean bluefin is thought to be as magnificent as the Alaska grizzly or the African leopard, will depletion of the world's oceans come to an end.

Discussion Questions

- What factors contribute to the lack of monitoring and regulation of tuna fishing around the world?

- If the most powerful incentive driving fishing practices in international waters is profit, is it reasonable to think that public awareness can reduce indifference enough to counter the rewards available to the international fishing industry? Why or why not?

- To what extent are the ethics of tuna ranching called into question in this article?

- How likely are the proposed reform measures to be effective, if adopted?

Writing Activities

- Evaluate the need for reform in the fishing industry, based on examples presented in the article. What are the most compelling reasons to impose stricter regulations on how much tuna is caught and the methods used, and how likely are they to be successfully implemented? (Suggestion: investigate/research the effects of initiatives in past decades motivated by a public outcry over dolphin mortality linked to tuna fishing.)

- Compare and/or contrast land-based industrial farming with the current methods of tuna fishing and ranching. What parallels can be drawn or differences highlighted?

- Should fishing be subject to the same protections that animal rights activists have achieved for livestock such as cattle, chickens, and pigs? Why or why not?

- Starting with the general reforms presented at the end of the article, write a proposal that offers reasonable steps that could help bring tuna fishing under control, taking into consideration the challenges presented by competing interests and other factors that would work directly against such reforms.

Collaborative Activities

- Working with a small group, list some basic strategies that could be effective in promoting more ethical fishing practices and raising consumer awareness of how their appetite for tuna contributes to the global fish crisis.

- Should Americans boycott the sale of tuna in grocery stores and restaurants? Discuss your views with a partner or two and then work together to evaluate the strength of each argument.

THE GULF OF OIL: THE DEEP DILEMMA

Bourne's report of the events surrounding the Gulf oil spill of 2010 provides some perspective on the disaster, highlighting a number of troubling decisions from within the oil industry, combined with a climate of poor oversight that led to the world's largest and most devastating oil spill.

As you read "The Gulf of Oil: The Deep Dilemma," consider the following questions:

- How and where have past oil spills occurred, and what was their environmental and economic impact?
- How well understood is the process of deep water drilling, and where have the largest risks been taken in expanding the scope of such methods to meet the demand for oil?
- Where does the potential for the most serious long-term effects of the spill lie?

Smoke rises from surface oil being burned by cleanup crews near the Deepwater Horizon blowout. The well spewed nearly five million barrels, making it the world's largest accidental marine oil spill. Eleven workers died in the explosion and flames that followed. On April 22 the rig sank.

THE GULF OF OIL: THE DEEP DILEMMA

"You could see the life draining out of it," says parish official P. J. Hahn, who impulsively rescued this severely oiled brown pelican on Queen Bess Island, La. The bird lived.

THE DEEP DILEMMA THE LARGEST U.S. OIL DISCOVERIES IN DECADES LIE IN THE DEPTHS OF THE GULF OF MEXICO—ONE OF

THE MOST DANGEROUS PLACES TO DRILL

ON THE PLANET.

Unflagging demand for oil propelled the industry into deep water but the blowout in the gulf forces the question:

Is it worth the risk?

On a blistering June day in Houma, Louisiana, the local offices of BP—now the *Deepwater Horizon* Incident Command Center—were swarming with serious men and women in brightly colored vests. Top BP managers and their consultants wore white, the logistics team wore orange, federal and state environmental officials wore blue. Reporters wore purple vests so their handlers could keep track of them. On the walls of the largest "war room," huge video screens flashed spill maps and response-vessel locations. Now and then one screen showed a World Cup soccer match.

Mark Ploen, the silver-haired deputy incident commander, wore a white vest. A 30-year veteran of oil spill wars, Ploen, a consultant, has helped clean up disasters around the world, from Alaska to the Niger Delta. He now found himself surrounded by men he'd worked with on the *Exxon Valdez* spill in Alaska two decades earlier. "It's like a high school reunion," he quipped.

Fifty miles offshore, a mile underwater on the seafloor, BP's Macondo well was spewing something like an *Exxon Valdez* every four days. In late April an explosive blowout of the well had turned the *Deepwater Horizon*, one of the world's most advanced drill rigs, into a pile of charred and twisted metal at the bottom of the sea. The industry had acted as if such a catastrophe would never occur. So had its regulators. Nothing like it had happened in the Gulf of Mexico since 1979, when a Mexican well called Ixtoc I blew out in the shallow waters of the Bay of Campeche. Drilling technology had become so good since then, and the demand for oil so irresistible, that oil companies had sailed right off the continental shelf into ever deeper waters.

To many people in industry and government, spills from tankers like the *Exxon Valdez*

Adapted from "The Gulf of Oil: The Deep Dilemma" by Joel K. Bourne Jr.: National Geographic Magazine, October 2010.

seemed a much larger threat. The Minerals Management Service (MMS), the federal agency that regulated offshore drilling, had claimed that the chances of a blowout were less than one percent, and that even if one did happen, it wouldn't release much oil. Big spills had become a rarity, said Ploen. "Until this one."

In the Houma building, more than a thousand people were trying to organize a cleanup unlike any the world had seen. Tens of thousands more were outside, walking beaches in white Tyvek suits, scanning the waters from planes and helicopters, and fighting the expanding slick with skimmers, repurposed fishing boats, and a deluge of chemical dispersants. Around the spot Ploen called simply "the source," a small armada bobbed in a sea of oil. A deafening roar came from the drill ship *Discoverer Enterprise* as it flared off methane gas captured from the runaway well. Flames also shot from another rig, the *Q4000*, which was burning oil and gas collected from a separate line attached to the busted blowout preventer. Nearby, two shrimp boats pulling fire boom were burning oil skimmed from the surface, creating a curving wall of flame and a towering plume of greasy, black smoke. Billions of dollars had already been spent. But millions of barrels of light, sweet crude were still snaking toward the barrier islands, marshes, and beaches of the Gulf of Mexico.

The waters of the Gulf below a thousand feet are a relatively new frontier for oilmen—and one of the toughest places on the planet to drill. The seafloor falls off the gently sloping continental shelf into jumbled basin-and-range-like terrain, with deep canyons, ocean ridges, and active mud volcanoes 500 feet high. More than 2,000 barrels of oil a day seep from scattered natural vents. But the commercial deposits lie deeply buried, often beneath layers of shifting salt that are prone to undersea earth-

> We have flipped design parameters around to the point that I got nervous. **This has been [a] nightmare well.**

quakes. Temperatures at the seafloor are near freezing, while the oil reservoirs can hit 400 degrees Fahrenheit; they're like hot, shaken soda bottles just waiting for someone to pop the top. Pockets of explosive methane gas and methane hydrates, frozen but unstable, lurk in the sediment, increasing the risk of a blowout.

For decades the exorbitant costs of drilling deep kept commercial rigs close to shore. But shrinking reserves, spiking oil prices, and spectacular offshore discoveries ignited a global rush into deep water. Recent finds in Brazil's Tupi and Guará fields could make that country one of the largest oil producers in the world. Similarly promising deepwater leases off Angola have excited bidding frenzies involving more than 20 companies.

In the Gulf of Mexico, the U.S. Congress encouraged companies to go deep as early as 1995. That year it passed a law forgiving royalties on deepwater oil fields leased between 1996 and 2000. A fleet of new rigs was soon punching holes all over the Gulf at a cost of up to a million dollars a day each. The number of leases sold in waters half a mile deep or more shot up from around 50 in 1994 to 1,100 in 1997.

As technology was taking drillers deeper, however, the methods for preventing blowouts and cleaning up spills did not keep pace. Since the early 2000s, reports from industry and academia warned of the increasing risk of deepwater blowouts, the fallibility of blowout preventers, and the difficulty of stopping a deepwater spill after it started—a special concern given that deepwater wells, because they're under such high pressure, can spout as much as 100,000 barrels a day.

The Minerals Management Service routinely downplayed such concerns. A 2007 agency study found that from 1992 to 2006, only 39 blowouts occurred during the drilling of more than 15,000 oil and gas wells in the Gulf. Few of them released much oil; only one resulted in a death. Most of the blowouts were stopped within a week, typically by pumping the wells full of heavy drilling mud or by shutting them down mechanically and diverting the gas bubble that had produced the dangerous "kick" in the first place.

Though blowouts were relatively rare, the MMS report did find a significant increase in the number associated with cementing, the process of pumping cement around the steel well casing (which surrounds the drill pipe) to fill the space between it and the wall of the borehole. In retrospect, that note of caution was ominous.

Some deepwater wells go in relatively easy. The Macondo well did not. BP hired Transocean, a Switzerland-based company, to drill the well. Transocean's first drill rig was knocked out of commission by Hurricane Ida after just a month. The *Deepwater Horizon* began its ill-fated effort in February 2010 and ran into problems almost from the start. In early March the drill pipe got stuck in the borehole, as did a tool sent down to find the stuck section; the drillers had to back out and drill around the obstruction. A BP email later released by Congress mentioned that the drillers were having "well-control" problems. Another email, from a consultant, stated, "We have flipped design parameters around to the point that I got nervous." A week before the explosion, a BP drilling engineer wrote, "This has been [a] nightmare well."

By April 20 the *Deepwater Horizon* was six weeks behind schedule, according to MMS documents, and the delay was costing BP more than half a million dollars a day. BP had chosen to drill the fastest possible way—using a well design known as a "long string" because it places strings of casing pipe between the oil reservoir and the wellhead. A long string generally has two barriers between the oil and the blowout preventer on the seafloor: a cement plug at the bottom of the well, and a metal seal, known as a lockdown sleeve, placed right at the wellhead. The lockdown sleeve had not been installed when the Macondo well blew out.

In addition, congressional investigators and industry experts contend that BP cut corners on its cement job. It failed to circulate heavy drilling mud outside the casing before cementing, a practice that helps the cement cure properly. It didn't put in enough centralizers—devices that ensure that the cement forms a complete seal around the casing. And it failed to run a test to see if the cement had bonded properly. Finally, just before the accident, BP replaced the heavy drilling mud in the well with much lighter seawater, as it prepared to finish and disconnect the rig from the well. BP declined to comment on these matters, citing the ongoing investigation.

All these decisions may have been perfectly legal, and they surely saved BP time and money—yet each increased the risk of a blowout. On the night of April 20, investigators suspect, a large gas bubble somehow infiltrated the casing, perhaps through gaps in the cement, and shot straight up. The blowout preventer should have stopped that powerful kick at the seafloor; its heavy hydraulic rams were supposed to shear the drill pipe like a soda straw, blocking the upward surge and protecting the rig above. But that fail-safe device had itself been beset by leaks and maintenance problems. When a geyser of drilling mud erupted onto the rig, all attempts to activate the blowout preventer failed.

The way BP drilled the Macondo well surprised Magne Ognedal, director general of the Petroleum Safety Authority Norway (PSA). The Norwegians have drilled high-temperature, high-pressure wells on their shallow continental shelf for decades, he said in a telephone interview, and haven't had a catastrophic blowout since 1985. After that incident, the PSA and the industry instituted a number of best practices for drilling exploration wells. These include riserless drilling from stations on the seafloor, which prevents oil and gas from flowing directly to a rig; starting a well with a small pilot hole through the sediment, which makes it easier to handle gas kicks; having a remote-controlled backup system for activating the blowout preventers; and most important, never allowing fewer than two barriers between the reservoir and the seafloor.

"The decisions [BP] made when they had indications that the well was not stable, the decision to have one long pipe, the decision to have only six centralizers instead of 21 to create the best possible cement job—some of these things were very surprising to us here," says Ognedal.

The roots of those decisions lie in BP's corporate history, says Robert Bea, a University of California, Berkeley expert in both technological disasters and offshore engineering. BP hired Bea in 2001 for advice on problems it faced after it took over the U.S. oil companies Amoco and ARCO. One problem, Bea says, was a loss of core competence: After the merger BP forced thousands of older, experienced oil field workers into early retirement. That decision, which made the company more dependent on contractors for engineering expertise, was a key ingredient in BP's "recipe for disaster," Bea says. Only a few of the 126 crew members on the *Deepwater Horizon* worked directly for BP.

The drilling operation itself was regulated by the MMS (which, in the wake of the accident, was reorganized and renamed the Bureau of Ocean Energy Management, Regulation, and Enforcement). In 2009 the MMS had been excoriated by the U.S. General Accounting Office for its lax oversight of offshore leases. That same year, under the new Obama Administration, the MMS rubber-stamped BP's initial drilling plan for the Macondo well. Using an MMS formula, BP calculated that the worst-case spill from the well would be 162,000 barrels a day—nearly three times the flow rate that actually occurred. In a separate spill-response plan for the whole Gulf, the company claimed that it could recover nearly 500,000 barrels a day using standard technology, so that even a worst-case spill would do minimal harm to the Gulf's fisheries and wildlife—including walruses, sea otters, and sea lions.

There are no walruses, sea otters, or sea lions in the Gulf. BP's plan also listed as an emergency responder a marine biologist who had been dead for years, and it gave the Web address of an entertainment site in Japan as an emergency source of spill-response equipment. The widely reported gaffes had appeared in other oil companies' spill-response plans as well. They had simply been cut and pasted from older plans prepared for the Arctic.

When the spill occurred, BP's response fell well short of its claims. Scientists on a federal task force said in early August that the blown-out well had disgorged as much as 62,000 barrels a day at the outset—an enormous flow rate, but far below BP's worst-case scenario. Mark Ploen estimated in June that on a good day his response teams, using skimmers brought in from around the world, were picking up 15,000 barrels. Simply burning the oil, a practice that had been used with the *Exxon Valdez* spill, had proved more effective. BP's burn fleet of 23 vessels included local shrimp boats that worked in pairs, corralling surface oil with long fire boom and then igniting it with homemade napalm. In one "monster burn" the team incinerated 16,000 barrels of oil in just over three hours.

"Shrimpers are naturals at doing this," said Neré Mabile, science and technology adviser for the burn team in Houma. "They know how to pull nets. They're seeing that every barrel we burn is a barrel that doesn't get to shore, doesn't affect the environment, doesn't affect people. And where's the safest place to burn this stuff? The middle of the Gulf of Mexico."

In June the *Discoverer Enterprise* and the *Q4000* began collecting oil directly at the busted blowout preventer, and by mid-July they had ramped up to 25,000 barrels a day—still far less, even when the efforts of the skimmers and the burn team were added, than the nearly 500,000 barrels a day BP had claimed it could remove. At that point the company finally succeeded in placing a tight cap on the well, halting the gusher after 12 weeks.

In 1990, after the *Exxon Valdez* spill, Congress's Office of Technology Assessment analyzed spill-response technologies and found them lacking. "Even the best national response system will have inherent practical limitations that will hinder spill-response efforts for catastrophic events—sometimes to a major extent," wrote OTA's director, John H. Gibbons. "For that reason it is important to pay at least equal attention to preventive measures as to response systems… The proverbial ounce of prevention is worth many, many pounds of cure."

When oil falls to the bottom, into the mud of lagoon or a marsh, it can hang around for decades, degrading the environment.

By early August BP seemed on the verge of plugging the Macondo well permanently with drilling mud and cement. The federal task force's estimate of the amount of oil released stood at 4.9 million barrels. Government scientists estimated that BP had removed a quarter of the oil. Another quarter had evaporated or dissolved into scattered molecules. But a third quarter had been dispersed in the water as small droplets, which might still be toxic to some organisms. And the last quarter—around five times the amount released by the *Exxon Valdez*—remained as slicks or sheens on the water or tar balls on the beaches. The *Deepwater Horizon* spill had become the largest accidental spill into the ocean in history, larger even than the Ixtoc I blowout in Mexico's Bay of Campeche in 1979. It is surpassed only by the intentional 1991 gulf war spill in Kuwait.

The Ixtoc spill devastated local fisheries and economies. Wes Tunnell remembers it well. The tall, 65-year-old coral reef expert at Texas A&M University–Corpus Christi earned his doctorate studying the reefs around Veracruz in the early 1970s, and he kept studying them for a decade after the spill coated them with oil. Tunnell wrote an early report on the impact there and on Padre Island in Texas. In early June, after the new disaster had once again raised the question of how long the impact of a spill can last, he returned to Enmedio Reef to see if any Ixtoc I oil remained. It took him three minutes of snorkeling to find some.

"Well, that was easy," he said.

Tunnell stood in the clear, waist-deep water of the protected reef lagoon holding what appeared to be a three-inch-thick slab of sandy gray clay. When he broke it in two, it was jet black on the inside, with the texture and smell of an asphalt brownie. Here on the lagoon side, where the reef looked gray and dead, the Ixtoc tar mat was still partially buried in the sediments. But on the ocean side of the reef, where winds and waves and currents were stronger, no oil remained. The lesson for Louisiana and the other Gulf states is clear, Tunnell thinks. Where there is wave energy and oxygen, sunlight and the Gulf's abundant oil-eating bacteria break it down fairly quickly. When oil falls to the bottom and gets entrained in low-oxygen sediments like those in a lagoon—or in a marsh—it can hang around for decades, degrading the environment.

Fishermen in the nearby village of Antón Lizardo hadn't forgotten the spill either. "The Ixtoc spill about destroyed all the reefs," said Gustavo Mateos Moutiel, a powerful man, now in his 60s, who wore the trademark straw hat of the Veracruzano fishermen. "Octopus gone. Urchins gone. Oysters gone. Conch gone. Fish almost all gone. Our families were hungry. The petroleum on the beach was halfway up our knees." Though some species, such as Bay of Campeche shrimps, recovered within a few years, Moutiel, along with several other fishermen who had gathered on the beach, said it took 15 to 20 years for their catches to return to normal. By then two-thirds of the fishermen in the village had found other jobs.

Even in the turbulent, highly oxygenated waters of France's Breton coast, it took at least seven years after the 1978 *Amoco Cadiz* spill for local marine species and Brittany's famed oyster farms to fully recover, according to French biologist Philippe *(Continued on page 110)*

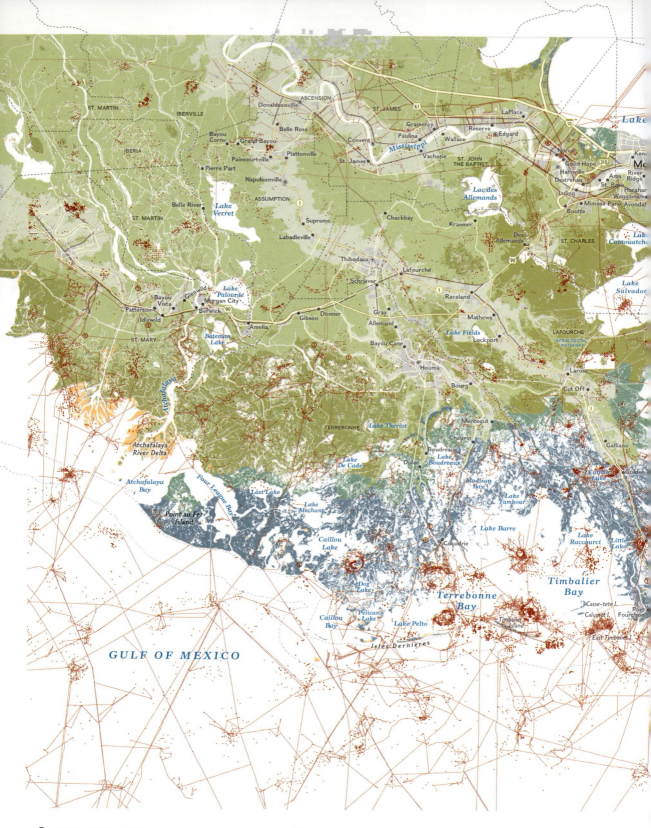

ST. MARTIN
IBERVILLE
Donaldsonville
ASCENSION
ST. JAMES
61
LaPlace
Lake
IBERIA
Bayou
Corne
Grand Bayou
Belle Rose
Gramercy
Paulina
Reserve
Edgard
10
Ken
ST. MARTIN
Paincourtville
Plattenville
Convent
Wallace
Norc
Me
Pierre Part
St. James
Vacherie
ST. JOHN
THE BAPTIST
Good Hope
310
Napoleonville
ASSUMPTION
Mississippi
Hahnville
River
Destrehan
Ridge
Ama
Luling
St. Ros
Hacahar
Waggaman
Belle River
Lake
Verret
Lac des
Allemands
Mimosa Park Avondal
Boutte
ST. MARTIN
Supreme
Chackbay
Kraemer
Des
Allemands
ST. CHARLES
Lake
Cataouatch
Labadieville
Thibodaux
Lafourche
90
Bayou
Vista
Glenfield
Lake
Palourde
Morgan City
Schriever
Raceland
Lake
Salvador
Patterson
Idlewild
Berwick
90
Donner
Gray
Mathews
Lake
Cataouatch
Amelia,
Gibson
Allemand
Lake Fields
Lockport
LAFOURCHE
Bateman
Lake
Bayou Cane
INTRACOASTAL
WATERWAY
Houma
Larose
Atchafalaya
Bourg
Cut Off
Atchafalaya
River Delta
TERREBONNE
Lake Theriot
Montegut
Galliano
Atchafalaya
Bay
Four League Bay
Lost Lake
Lake
De Cade
Dulac
Boudreaux
Lake
Boudreaux
Chauvin
Madison
Bay
Cajun
Lake
Golden
Point au Fer
Island
Lake
Mechant
Lake
Tambour
Caillou
Lake
Cocodrie
Lake Barre
Lake
Raccourci
Little
Lake
Dog
Lake
Terrebonne
Bay
Casse-tête I.
Caillou
Bay
Pelican
Lake
Lake Pelto
Timbalier
Island
Calumet I.
Port
Fourchon
Istes Dernieres
East Timbalier I.
GULF OF MEXICO

---

1 NEW DELTA LAND

On the Louisiana coast, new land is being formed in the Atchafalaya River Delta, as river sediment replenishes wetlands.
Large-scale diversions of Mississippi and Atchafalaya river
waters are proposed to feed the marshes but could interfere
with deepwater navigation and key species like oysters.

2 OIL INFRASTRUCTURE

Since the 1940s, oil companies have built thousands of drilling plat-
forms along Louisiana's coast. Tens of thousands of pipelines connect those rigs to shore. The oil industry pumps $70 billion a year
into the state; its rigs create a secure habitat for fish. But pipeline
canals speed erosion, and the risk of spills is ever present.

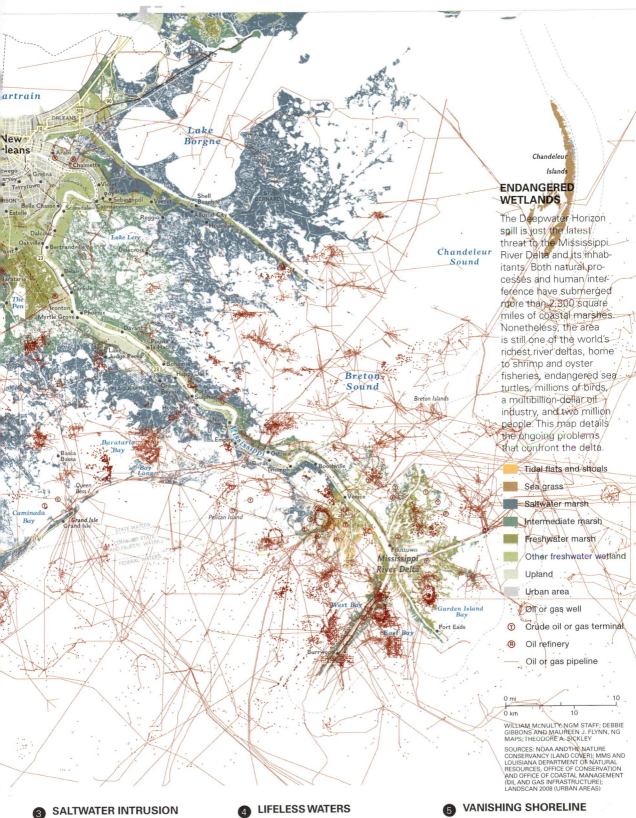

ENDANGERED WETLANDS

The Deepwater Horizon spill is just the latest threat to the Mississippi River Delta and its inhabitants. Both natural processes and human interference have submerged more than 2,300 square miles of coastal marshes. Nonetheless, the area is still one of the world's richest river deltas, home to shrimp and oyster fisheries, endangered sea turtles, millions of birds, a multibillion-dollar oil industry, and two million people. This map details the ongoing problems that confront the delta.

Tidal flats and shoals
Sea grass
Saltwater marsh
Intermediate marsh
Freshwater marsh
Other freshwater wetland
Upland
Urban area
Oil or gas well
(T) Crude oil or gas terminal
(R) Oil refinery
Oil or gas pipeline

0 mi _____ 10
0 km _____ 10

WILLIAM McNULTY, NGM STAFF; DEBBIE GIBBONS AND MAUREEN J. FLYNN, NG MAPS; THEODORE A. SICKLEY

SOURCES: NOAA AND THE NATURE CONSERVANCY (LAND COVER); MMS AND LOUISIANA DEPARTMENT OF NATURAL RESOURCES, OFFICE OF CONSERVATION AND OFFICE OF COASTAL MANAGEMENT (OIL AND GAS INFRASTRUCTURE); LANDSCAN 2008 (URBAN AREAS)

③ SALTWATER INTRUSION

As wetlands sink and fragment, salt water slips farther inland, killing the freshwater marshes that make up 81 percent of Mississippi River Delta wetlands, home to diverse plants and animals. Canals dug to accommodate oil pipelines and ships speed salt water inland with the tides; faster currents increase erosion.

④ LIFELESS WATERS

Each summer a "dead zone" of oxygen-starved water develops along the coast. Algae blooms, fed by nitrogen and phosphorus from animal waste and fertilizers from midwestern farms, create this zone, which averages about 6,000 square miles. The dead zone threatens the Gulf's rich coastal fisheries.

⑤ VANISHING SHORELINE

Fragile marshland soils need replenishment with sediment and nutrients, but levees built for flood control and navigation shoot those substances out to sea. Draining swamps for development and pumping groundwater cause ground to subside, drowning marsh plants and creating expanses of open water.

AN OILY STAIN

Winds and currents spread surface oil, contaminating more than 625 miles of coastline, most in Louisiana. The spill prompted a fishing ban in one-third of federal waters (partly rescinded in late July) and a massive and ongoing cleanup effort. Experts believe much of the oil never reached the surface and remains in voluminous and elusive underwater plumes.

THE BATTERED GULF COAST

Two centuries of efforts to tame the Mississippi River with levees, pumps, and channels have left its vast wetlands ecosystem dwindling and on the verge of collapse. "We know there was a crisis in the Gulf prior to what happened April 20," Tom Strickland, an assistant secretary of the interior, said after the Deepwater Horizon spill. Coastal-restoration plans have been authorized by Congress but are not yet under way. They include breaking open levees to restore the flow of rivers to marshlands. Environmentalists are lobbying to apply oil spill penalty funds to restoration.

(Continued from page 107) Bodin. An expert on marine copepods, Bodin studied the long-term effects of the spill from the grounded tanker. He believes the impact will be far worse in the generally calmer, lower-oxygen waters of the Gulf, particularly because of the heavy use of the dispersant Corexit 9500. BP has said the chemical is no more toxic than dishwashing liquid, but it was used extensively on the *Amoco Cadiz* spill, and Bodin found it to be more toxic to marine life than the oil itself. "The massive use of Corexit 9500 in the Gulf is catastrophic for the phytoplankton, zooplankton, and larvae," he says. "Moreover, currents will drive the dispersant and the oil plumes everywhere in the Gulf."

In May, scientists in the Gulf began tracking plumes of methane and oil droplets drifting up to 30 miles from the broken well, at depths of 3,000 to 4,000 feet. One of those

Canals carved through Golden Meadow, La., and elsewhere hold pipelines that deliver oil and gas from offshore wells. This chopping up of the wetlands is one of many forces contributing to the decline of the Mississippi Delta.

scientists was University of Georgia biogeo-chemist Mandy Joye, who has spent years studying hydrocarbon vents and brine seeps in the deep Gulf. She found a plume the size of Manhattan, and its methane levels were the highest she had ever measured in the Gulf. As bacteria feast on spilled oil and methane, they deplete the water of oxygen; at one point Joye found oxygen levels dangerously low for life in a water layer 600 feet thick, at depths where fish usually live. Since waters in the deep Gulf mix very slowly, she said, such depleted zones could persist for decades.

BP was using old DC-3s set up like giant crop dusters to spray Corexit 9500 onto surface slicks. But for the world's first major deepwater spill, the company also got permission from the U.S. Environmental Protection Agency and the Coast Guard to pump hundreds of thousands of gallons of dispersant directly into the oil and gas spewing from the well, a mile beneath the surface. That helped create the deepwater plumes.

"The whole goal is to keep oil off the beaches, because that's what drives the economy," Joye said one day in June as she ran samples through her gas chromatograph aboard the R.V. *F. G. Walton Smith.* The little research ship was bobbing in an oily sheen a few miles from the busted well. "But now you've got all this material in the water column that no one is seeing and that you can't get rid of. If oil gets to the surface, about 40 percent evaporates. You can skim it, you can burn it, you can do something with it. But these tiny particles in the water column will persist for God knows how long."

Oceanographer Ian MacDonald at Florida State University worries not only about the plumes but also about the sheer volume of spilled oil. He believes it could have a major impact on the overall productivity of the Gulf—not just on pelicans and shrimps in the Louisiana marshes, but on creatures throughout the region, everything from zooplankton to sperm whales. He's particularly concerned about bluefin tuna, which spawn only in the Gulf and in the Mediterranean; the tuna population was already crashing due to overfishing. "There is a tremendous amount of highly toxic material in the water column, both at the surface and below, moving around in one of the most productive ocean basins in the world," MacDonald said.

During their June cruise Joye's team sampled water within a mile of the *Discoverer Enterprise*, close enough to hear the apocalyptic roar of its huge methane flare. Researchers and crew members stood on the back deck of the *Walton Smith* and quietly took pictures. The caustic vapors of oil, diesel, and asphalt burned their lungs. As far as the eye could see, the cobalt blue waters of the deep Gulf were stained brownish red. When Joye went back inside she was in a pensive mood.

"The *Deepwater Horizon* incident is a direct consequence of our global addiction to oil," she said. "Incidents like this are inevitable as we drill in deeper and deeper waters. We're playing a very dangerous game here. If this isn't a call to green power, I don't know what is."

Americans burn nearly 20 million barrels of oil a day. In early August the U.S. Senate adjourned for the summer without taking up an energy bill.

Discussion Questions

- How does Joel K. Bourne Jr. use descriptive language and detail to paint a vivid picture of the spill situation, and what is his purpose in doing so?

- In what ways do the decisions made by BP in drilling methods and safety highlight a lack of concern about risk, and what factors can be linked to these attitudes?

- What are the most important factors contributing to the disaster? Which shortcomings in engineering, planning, oversight, and response stand out the most, and why?

- Specifically, when and where has the oil industry missed opportunities to adapt to lessons that might have been learned from past accidents?

Writing Activities

- Write an essay that analyzes the responsibilities of the oil industry, specifically as they relate to the causes of the Gulf oil spill, the response, the clean up, and the restoration of economic and environmental systems in the region. Provide your overall assessment of the strengths and weaknesses shown in these areas.

- Research the history of the Louisiana coast and write an informative essay that examines the state of its wetlands before and after the Gulf oil spill. What environmental factors pose the most concern, in light of recent and historical events?

- Construct a well-reasoned argument for or against deep water drilling off the U.S. coast, using effective examples to illustrate your points. Include a reference to at least one other reading in this collection as you build your supporting points.

- Interview at least two people from different backgrounds who followed the Gulf oil spill closely or were impacted in some way by the disaster. Taking into account their experiences and any of your own experiences concerning the spill, write an essay that analyzes the impact of the spill on a personal level and offers your assessment of how the disaster has been handled by BP or any other agencies involved in responding to the human toll the spill has taken.

Collaborative Activities

- In a small group, examine the past oil spills mentioned in the article and the underlying problems linked to the catastrophic BP spill. Working together, identify some common elements and review these carefully in order to find areas where preventative measures might have been taken.

- As a group, explore the potential impact on the Gulf region's economy and the environment. Using details provided in the article as a reference, examine the responsibilities of industry, government, and science to minimize the chances that an accident of this magnitude would happen. After discussing those whom you hold most accountable, summarize your reasons.

THE 21ST CENTURY GRID

Joel Achenbach's title for this essay is "The 21st Century Grid" with the subtitle "Can we fix the infrastructure that powers our lives?" Take note of this central question and his tone as you read about the aging system that transmits the energy that powers our lives.

As you read "The 21st Century Grid," consider the following questions:

- What is a "smarter" grid, and why, according to the author, is it needed at this time?
- In what ways does our consumption of electricity go unnoticed, and to what extent can increased awareness help us use it more efficiently?

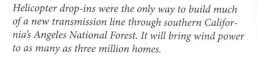

Helicopter drop-ins were the only way to build much of a new transmission line through southern California's Angeles National Forest. It will bring wind power to as many as three million homes.

THE 21ST CENTURY GRID

Photographs by Joe McNally

From PlayStations to iMacs, the small electronic devices that appeal to Corbin Stafford (at right) and Aaron Bear Paul, of Boulder, Colorado, have a big impact. Worldwide they account for about 15 percent of residential electricity consumption.

CAN WE FIX THE INFRASTRUCTURE
THAT POWERS
OUR LIVES?

We are creatures of the grid. We are embedded in it and empowered by it. The sun used to govern our lives, but now, thanks to the grid, darkness falls at our convenience. During the Depression, when power lines first electrified rural America, a farmer in Tennessee rose in church one Sunday and said—power companies love this story— "The greatest thing on earth is to have the love of God in your heart, and the next greatest thing is to have electricity in your house." He was talking about a few lightbulbs and maybe a radio. He had no idea.

Juice from the grid now penetrates every corner of our lives, and we pay no more attention to it than to the oxygen in the air. Until something goes wrong, that is, and we're suddenly in the dark, fumbling for flashlights and candles, worrying about the frozen food in what used to be called (in pre-grid days) the icebox. Or until the batteries run dry in our laptops or smart phones, and we find ourselves scouring the dusty corners of airports for an outlet, desperate for the magical power of electrons.

But the first thing a smart grid will do, if we let it, is turn us into savvier consumers of electricity.

The grid is wondrous. And yet—in part because we've paid so little attention to it, engineers tell us—it's not the grid we need for the 21st century. It's too old. It's reliable but not reliable enough, especially in the United States, especially for our mushrooming population of finicky digital devices. Blackouts, brownouts, and other power outs cost Americans an estimated $80 billion a year. And at the same time that it needs to become more reliable, the grid needs dramatic upgrading to handle a different kind of power, a greener kind. That means, among other things, more transmission lines to carry wind power and solar power from remote places to big cities.

Most important, the grid must get smarter. The precise definition of "smart" varies from one engineer to the next. The gist is that a smart grid would be more automated and more "self-healing," and so less prone to failure. It would be more tolerant of small-scale, variable power sources such as solar panels

Adapted from "The 21st Century Grid" by Joel Achenbach: National Geographic Magazine, July 2010.

and wind turbines, in part because it would even out fluctuations by storing energy—in the batteries of electric cars, according to one speculative vision of the future, or perhaps in giant caverns filled with compressed air.

But the first thing a smart grid will do, if we let it, is turn us into savvier consumers of electricity. We'll become aware of how much we're consuming and cut back, especially at moments of peak demand, when electricity costs most to produce. That will save us and the utilities money—and incidentally reduce pollution. In a way, we'll stop being mere passive consumers of electrons. In the 21st century we'll become active participants in the management of this vast and seemingly unknowable network that makes our civilization possible.

So maybe it's time we got to know it.

There are grids today on six continents, and someday Europe's may reach across the Mediterranean into Africa to carry solar power from the Sahara to Scandinavia. In Canada and the United States the grid carries a million megawatts across tens of millions of miles of wire. It has been called the world's biggest machine. The National Academy of Engineering calls it the greatest engineering achievement of the last century.

Thomas Edison, already famous for his lightbulb, organized the birth of the grid in 1881, digging up lower Manhattan to lay down copper wires inside brick tunnels. He constructed a power plant, the Pearl Street Station, in the shadow of the Brooklyn Bridge. On September 4, 1882, in the office of tycoon J. P. Morgan, Edison threw a switch. Hundreds of his bulbs lit up Drexel, Morgan & Co. and other offices nearby.

It took decades for electricity to expand from factories and mansions into the homes of the middle class. In 1920 electricity still

> **The electrical grid is basically 1960s technology. The Internet has passed it by. The meter on the side of your house is 1920s technology.**

accounted for less than 10 percent of the U.S. energy supply. But inexorably it infiltrated everyday life. Unlike coal, oil, or gas, electricity is clean at the point of use. There is no noise, except perhaps a faint hum, no odor, and no soot on the walls. When you switch on an electric lamp, you don't think of the huge, sprawling power plant that's generating the electricity (noisily, odoriferously, sootily) many miles away. Refrigerators replaced iceboxes, air conditioners replaced heat prostration, and in 1956 the electric can opener completed our emergence from the dark ages. Today about 40 percent of the energy we use goes into making electricity.

At first, utilities were local operations that ran the generating plant and the distribution. A patchwork of mini-grids formed across the United States. In time the utilities realized they could improve reliability and achieve economies of scale by linking their transmission networks. After the massive Northeast blackout of 1965, much of the control of the grid shifted to regional operators spanning many states. Yet today there is still no single grid in the United States there are three nearly independent ones—the Eastern, Western, and Texas Interconnections.

They function with antiquated technology. The parts of the grid you come into contact with are symptomatic. How does the power company measure your electricity usage? With a meter reader—a human being who goes to your home or business and reads the dials on a meter. How does the power company learn that you've lost power? When you call on the phone. In general, utilities don't have enough instantaneous information on the flow of current through their lines—many of those lines don't carry any data—and people and slow mechanical switches are too involved in controlling that flow.

"The electrical grid is still basically 1960s technology," says physicist Phillip F. Schewe, author of *The Grid*. "The Internet has passed it by. The meter on the side of your house is 1920s technology." Sometimes that quaintness becomes a problem. On the grid these days, things can go bad very fast.

When you flip a light switch, the electricity that zips into the bulb was created just a fraction of a second earlier, many miles away. Where it was made, you can't know, because hundreds of power plants spread over many states are all pouring their output into the same communal grid. Electricity can't be stored on a large scale with today's technology; it has to be used instantly. At each instant there has to be a precise balance between generation and demand over the whole grid. In control rooms around the grid, engineers constantly monitor the flow of electricity, trying to keep voltage and frequency steady and to avoid surges that could damage both their customers' equipment and their own.

When I flip a switch at my house in Washington, D.C., I'm dipping into a giant pool of electricity called the PJM Interconnection. PJM is one of several regional operators that make up the Eastern grid; it covers the District of Columbia and 13 states, from the Mississippi River east to New Jersey and all the way down to the Outer Banks of North Carolina. It's an electricity market that keeps supply and demand almost perfectly matched—every day, every minute, every fraction of a second—among hundreds of producers and distributors and 51 million people, via 56,350 miles of high-voltage transmission lines.

One of PJM's new control centers is an hour north of Philadelphia. Last February I went to visit it with Ray E. Dotter, a company spokesman. Along the way Dotter identified the power lines we passed under. There was a pair of 500-kilovolt lines linking the Limerick nuclear plant with the Whitpain substation. Then a 230-kilovolt line. Then another.

Burying the ungainly lines is prohibitively expensive except in dense cities. "There's a need to build new lines," Dotter said. "But no matter where you propose them, people don't want them."

Dotter pulled off the turnpike in the middle of nowhere. A communications tower poked above the treetops. We drove onto a compound surrounded by a security fence. Soon we were in the bunker, built by AT&T during the Cold War to withstand anything but a direct nuclear hit and recently purchased by PJM to serve as its new nerve center.

Computers take data from 65,000 points on the system, he explained. They track the thermal condition of the wires; too much power flowing through a line can overheat it, causing the line to expand and sag dangerously. PJM engineers try to keep the current alternating at a frequency of precisely 60 hertz. As demand increases, the frequency drops, and if it drops below 59.95 hertz, PJM sends a message to power plants asking for more output. If the frequency increases above 60.05 hertz, they ask the plants to reduce output. It sounds simple, but keeping your balance on a tightrope might sound simple too until you try it. In the case of the grid, small events not under the control of the operators can quickly knock down the whole system.

Which brings us to August 14, 2003. Most of PJM's network escaped the disaster, which started near Cleveland. The day was hot; the air conditioners were humming. Shortly after 1 p.m EDT, grid operators at First Energy, the regional utility, called power plants to plead for more volts. At 1:36 p.m. on the shore of Lake Erie, a power station whose operator had just promised to "push it to my max max" responded by crashing. Electricity surged into northern Ohio from elsewhere to take up the slack.

At 3:05 a 345-kilovolt transmission line near the town of Walton Hills picked that moment to short out on a tree that hadn't been trimmed. That failure diverted *(Continued on page 124)*

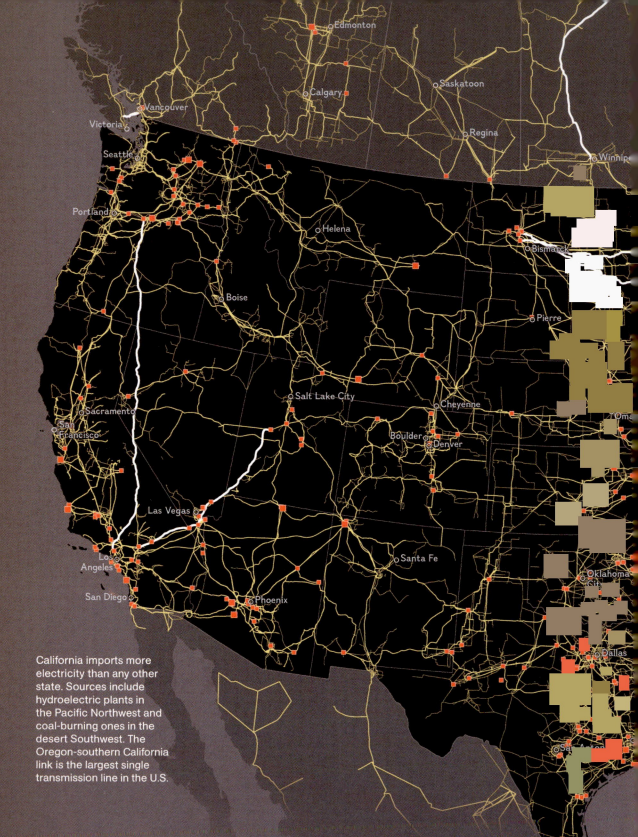

California imports more electricity than any other state. Sources include hydroelectric plants in the Pacific Northwest and coal-burning ones in the desert Southwest. The Oregon-southern California link is the largest single transmission line in the U.S.

THE GRID TODAY

More than 150,000 miles of high-voltage transmission lines carry power from 5,400 generating plants owned by more than 3,000 utilities. Most of those lines carry alternating current (AC), but 1.9 percent of them carry direct current (DC), which loses less power over very long distances. The grid works 99.97 percent of the time—but power interruptions still cost the U.S. economy about $80 billion each

2003 BLACKOUT
Eight states and Ontario, Canada, (purple area) lost power in the 2003 blackout. It was a dramatic reminder of the vulnerability of the existing grid.

Blackout of 2003

Thunder Bay

Lake Superior

Charlottetown

Quebec

Halifax

Minneapolis

Lake Michigan

L. Huron

L. Ontario

Milwaukee

Toronto

Niagara Falls

Buffalo

Montreal

Ottawa

Boston

Des Moines

Chicago

Detroit

Cleveland

L. Erie

Walton Hills

New York

Pittsburgh

Philadelphia

Cincinnati

Washington, D.C.

St. Louis

Norfolk

Raleigh

Nashville

Memphis

Atlanta

Jackson

New Orleans

Tampa

Miami

Power plants, 2009
(in megawatts)

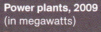

- ■ Greater than 2,000
- ■ 250 to 2,000

Transmission lines, 2009
(direct or alternating current, in kilovolts)

— DC (variable)
— AC 735-999
— AC 230-734
— AC 100-229*

*TRANSMISSION LINES BELOW 100 KV CAPACITY ARE NOT SHOWN.

MARTIN GAMACHE AND SAM PEPPLE, NGM STAFF

SOURCES: NORTH AMERICAN ELECTRIC RELIABILITY CORPORATION; PLATTS, A DIVISION OF MCGRAW-HILL COMPANIES (GENERATION AND TRANSMISSION INFRASTRUCTURE); U.S.-CANADA POWER SYSTEM OUTAGE TASK FORCE; U.S. DEPARTMENT OF ENERGY

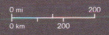

0 mi   200
0 km   200

year. Moreover, our electricity is anything but clean. Most of it comes from burning fossil fuels, about half of it from coal. Hydroelectric, wind, and solar power account for less than 8 percent. The infrastructure perpetuates this: Texas currently has more wind-generation capacity than the grid can handle.

Edmonton

Calgary

Saskatoon

Regina

Winnipeg

Vancouver

Victoria

Seattle

Portland

Helena

Bismarck

Boise

Pierre

Salt Lake City

Cheyenne

Omaha

Des Moin

San Francisco

Sacramento

Boulder

Denver

Las Vegas

TEHACHAPI PROJECT

Los Angeles

SOUTHWEST AREA NATL. INTEREST ELECTRIC TRANSMISSION CORRIDOR

San Diego

Phoenix

Santa Fe

Clovis

Oklahoma City

Dallas

Abilene

Houston

San Antonio

California's renewable energy law has led to a burst of wind and solar projects—as well as plans for high-voltage DC lines to bring renewable energy in from elsewhere. One idea: a 650-mile submarine cable to import hydroelectricity from Oregon.

Proposed new transmission lines, including the Tres Amigas project near Clovis, New Mexico, could help Texas deliver its abundant wind energy to far-flung cities in the East and West.

NEW LINES ON THE GRID

Superimposing the grid of the future on the current one will not be cheap. Nearly $30 billion in new generation plants and high-voltage transmission lines are planned in the West alone. Both federal subsidies and state-set goals for renewable energy—30 percent in New York by 2015; 33 percent in California by 2020—are encouraging the construction of new transmission lines, which in some cases are also needed to improve the reliability of the grid. Reliability should also rise, along with energy efficiency, as the grid gets "smarter"—that is, as utilities increase their ability to monitor the flow of electricity from generator to consumer.

CONGESTED AREAS

The federal government has defined two "national corridors" (pink, below), in the mid-Atlantic and Southwest, where transmission lines are most in need of relief.

Thunder Bay

Charlottetown

Quebec

Halifax

Montreal

Ottawa

Boston

Toronto

Niagara Falls
Buffalo

Milwaukee

Detroit

Cleveland
Walton
Hills

New York

Chicago

Pittsburgh

Philadelphia

MID-ATLANTIC AREA
NATIONAL INTEREST ELECTRIC
TRANSMISSION CORRIDOR

Cincinnati

Washington, D.C.

Norfolk

Raleigh

Nashville

Memphis

Atlanta

Turbines submerged along the Mississippi and its tributaries have been proposed as a way to generate hydroelectricity without dams.

Jackson

New Orleans

Tampa

Miami

Suitable for large wind or solar projects

Solar* Wind** Wind and solar Less suitable

The Southwest is a solar-power hotbed; the Great Plains are reliably windswept. Other regions have less uniform supplies of sun and wind.

Proposed power plants

Capacity (in megawatts)

☐ Greater than 2,000
☐ 500-2,000
▫ Less than 500

Fuel

- ☐ Wind
- ☐ Hydro
- ☐ Solar
- ■ Nonrenewable†
- ☐ Nuclear
- ☐ Other†

Proposed transmission lines
(in kilovolts)

— DC (variable)
— AC 735-999
— AC 345-734
— AC 230-344

* MINIMUM ANNUAL AVERAGE OF 18.6 WATTS PER SQUARE FOOT

** MINIMUM ANNUAL AVERAGE SPEED OF 14.6 MILES AN HOUR AT 262 FEET ABOVEGROUND

† NONRENEWABLE INCLUDES COAL, KEROSENE, NATURAL GAS, AND PROPANE. OTHER INCLUDES BIOMASS AND GEOTHERMAL.

MARTIN GAMACHE AND SAM PEPPLE, NGM STAFF
SOURCES: STIER (SOLAR AND WIND DATA ANALYSIS);
VENTYX (GENERATION AND TRANSMISSION
INFRASTRUCTURE); U.S. DEPARTMENT OF ENERGY

(Continued from page 119) electricity onto other lines, overloading and overheating them. One by one, like firecrackers, those lines sagged, touched trees, and short-circuited.

Grid operators have a term for this: "cascading failures." The First Energy operators couldn't see the cascade coming because an alarm system had also failed. At 4:06 a final line failure sent the cascade to the East Coast. With no place to park their electricity, 265 power plants shut down. The largest blackout in North American history descended on 50 million people in eight states and Ontario.

At the Consolidated Edison control center in lower Manhattan, operators remember that afternoon well. Normally the power load there dips gradually, minute by minute, as workers in the city turn off their lights and computers and head home. Instead, at 4:13 p.m. lights went out in the control room itself. The operators thought: 9/11. Then the phone rang, and it was the New York Stock Exchange. "What's going on?" someone asked. The operators knew at once that the outage was citywide.

There was no stock trading then, no banking, and no manufacturing; restaurants closed, workers were idled, and everyone just sat on the stoops of their apartment buildings. It took a day and a half to get power back, one feeder and substation at a time. The blackout cost six billion dollars. It also alarmed Pentagon and Homeland Security officials. They fear the grid is indeed vulnerable to terrorist attack, not just to untrimmed trees.

The blackout and global warming have provided a strong impetus for grid reform. The federal government is spending money on the grid—the economic-stimulus package allocated $4.5 billion to smart grid projects and another six billion dollars or so to new transmission lines. Nearly all the major utilities have smart grid efforts of their own.

> There's a need to build new lines, but no matter where you propose them, **people don't want them.**

A smarter grid would help prevent blackouts in two ways. Faster, more detailed feedback on the status of the grid would help operators stay ahead of a failure cascade. Supply and demand would also be easier to balance, because controllers would be able to tinker with both. "The way we designed and built the power system over the last hundred years—basically the way Edison and Westinghouse designed it— we create the supply side," says Steve Hauser of the U.S. Department of Energy's National Renewable Energy Laboratory (NREL) near Boulder, Colorado. "We do very little to control demand."

Working with the NREL, Xcel Energy has brought smart grid technology to Boulder. The first step is the installation of smart meters that transmit data over fiber-optic cable (it could also be done wirelessly) to the power company. Those meters allow consumers to see what electricity really costs at different times of day; it costs more to generate during times of peak load, because the utilities have to crank up auxiliary generators that aren't as efficient as the huge ones they run 24/7.

When consumers are given a price difference, they can choose to use less of the expensive electricity and more of the cheap kind. They can run clothes dryers and dishwashers at night, for instance. The next step is to let grid operators choose. Instead of only increasing electricity supply to meet demand, the operators could also reduce demand. On sweltering summer days the smart grid could automatically turn up thermostats and refrigerators a bit—with the prior agreement of the homeowners of course.

"Demand management" saves energy, but it could also help the grid handle renewable energy sources. One of the biggest problems with renewables like solar and wind power is that they're intermittent. They're not always available when demand peaks. Reducing the peak alleviates that problem. You can even imagine programming smart appliances to operate only when solar or wind power is available.

Some countries, such as Italy and Sweden, are ahead of the United States in upgrading their electrical intelligence. The Boulder project went online earlier this year, but only about 10 percent of U.S. customers have even the most primitive of smart meters, Hauser estimates.

"It's expensive," he says. "Utilities are used to spending 40 bucks on an old mechanical meter that's got spinning dials. A smart meter with a software chip, plus the wireless communication, might cost $200—five times as much. For utilities, that's huge." The Boulder project has cost Xcel Energy nearly three times what it expected. Earlier this year the utility raised rates to try to recoup some of those costs.

Although everyone acknowledges the need for a better, smarter, cleaner grid, the paramount goal of the utility industry continues to be cheap electricity. In the United States about half of it comes from burning coal. Coal-powered generators produce a third of the mercury emissions in the United States, a third of our smog, two-thirds of our sulfur dioxide, and nearly a third of our planet-warming carbon dioxide—around 2.5 billion metric tons a year, by the most recent estimate.

Not counting hydroelectric plants, only about 3 percent of U.S. electricity comes from renewable energy. The main reason is that coal-fired electricity costs a few cents a kilowatt-hour, and renewables cost substantially more. Generally they're competitive only with the help of government regulations or tax incentives. Utility executives are a conservative bunch. Their job is to keep the lights on. Radical change makes them nervous; things they can't control, such as government policies, make them nervous. "They tend to like stable environments," says Ted Craver, head of Edison International, a utility conglomerate, "because they tend to make very large capital investments and eat that cooking for 30 or 40 or 50 years."

So windmills worry them. A utility executive might look at one and think: What if the wind doesn't blow? Or look at solar panels and think: What if it gets cloudy? A smart grid alone can't solve the intermittence problem. The ultimate solution is finding ways to store large amounts of electricity for a rainy, windless day.

Actually the United States can already store around 2 percent of its summer power output—and Europe even more—behind hydroelectric dams. At night, when electricity is cheaper, some utilities use it to pump water back uphill into their reservoirs, essentially storing electricity for the next day. A small power plant in Alabama does something similar; it pumps air into an underground cavern at night, compressing it to more than a thousand pounds per square inch. During the day the compressed air comes rushing out and spins a turbine. In the past year the Department of Energy has awarded stimulus money to several utilities for compressed-air projects. One project in Iowa would use wind energy to compress the air.

Another way to store electricity, of course, is in batteries. For the moment, it makes sense on a large scale only in extreme situations. For example, the remote city of Fairbanks, Alaska, relies on a huge nickel-cadmium, emergencybackup battery. It's the size of a football field.

Lithium-ion batteries have more long-term potential—especially the ones in electric or plug-in-hybrid cars. PJM is already paying researchers at the University of Delaware $200 a month to store juice in three electric Toyotas as a test of the idea. The cars draw energy from the grid when they're charging, but when PJM needs electricity to keep its frequency stable, the cars are plugged in to give some back. Many thousands of cars, the researchers say, could someday function as a kind of collective battery for the entire grid. They would draw electricity when wind and solar plants are generating, and then feed some back when the wind dies down or night falls or the sun goes behind clouds. The Boulder smart grid is designed to allow such two-way flow.

To accommodate green energy, the grid needs not only more storage but more highvoltage power lines. There aren't enough running to the places where it's easy to generate the energy. To connect wind farms in Kern County with the Los Angeles area, Southern California Edison, a subsidiary of Edison International, is building 250 miles of them, known as the Tehachapi Renewable Transmission Project. A California law requires utilities to generate at least 20 percent of their electricity from renewable sources as of this year.

Green energy would also get a boost if there were more and bigger connections between the three quasi-independent grids in the United States West Texas is a Saudi Arabia of wind, but the Texas Interconnection by itself can't handle all that energy. A proposed project called the Tres Amigas Superstation would allow Texas wind—and Arizona sun—to supply Chicago or Los Angeles. Near Clovis, New Mexico, where the three interconnections already nearly touch, they would be joined together by a loop of five-gigawatt-capacity superconducting cable. The three grids would become, in effect, one single grid, national and almost rational.

The grid is a kind of parallel world that props up our familiar one but doesn't map onto it perfectly. It's a human construction that has grown organically, like a city or a government—what technical people call a kludge. A kludge is an awkward, inelegant contraption that somehow works. The U.S. grid works well by most

> **A**lthough everyone acknowledges the need for **a better, smarter, cleaner grid,** the paramount goal of the utility industry continues to be cheap electric.

measures, most of the time; electricity is abundant and cheap.

It's just that our measures have changed, and so the grid must too. The power industry, says Ted Craver of Edison International, faces "more change in the next ten years than we've seen in the last hundred." But at least now the rest of us are starting to pay attention.

CAN SOLAR SAVE US? PROBABLY. EVENTUALLY. WITH LOTS OF GOVERNMENT HELP.

The sun is a utopian fuel: limitless, ubiquitous, and clean. Surely someday we'll give up on coal, oil, and gas—so hard on the climate, so unequally distributed worldwide—and go straight to the energy source that made fossil fuels. In a few sunny places where electric rates are high, like Italy and Hawaii, solar energy is already on the verge of being competitive. But in most places the sun remains by far the most expensive source of electric power—typically in the United States it costs several times more than natural gas or coal—which is why it still supplies only a fraction of a percent of our needs.

That won't change fast unless governments give solar a big boost. President Barack Obama campaigned with a pledge to institute a federal "renewable portfolio standard" requiring utilities to generate a quarter of their electricity from renewables by 2025. Yet even if Congress enacted that ambitious law, coal would still dominate the nation's electricity portfolio two decades from now, and solar energy would

---

Adapted from "Can Solar Save Us?" by Chris Carroll: National Geographic Magazine, September 2009.

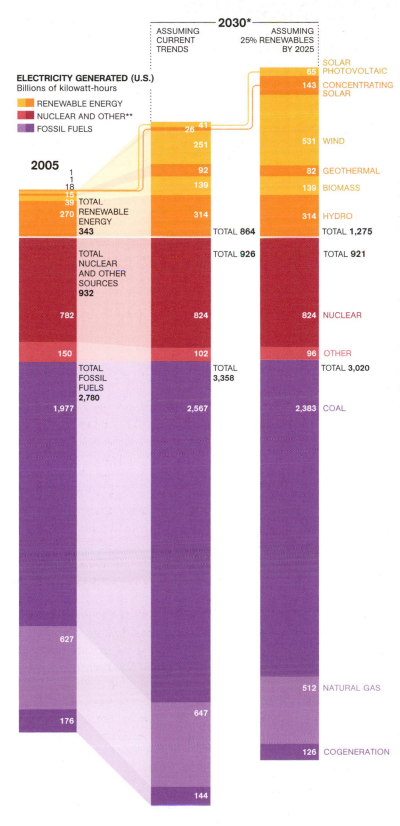

ELECTRICITY GENERATED (U.S.)
Billions of kilowatt-hours

- 🟧 RENEWABLE ENERGY
- 🟥 NUCLEAR AND OTHER**
- 🟪 FOSSIL FUELS

2005

2030*

ASSUMING CURRENT TRENDS

ASSUMING 25% RENEWABLES BY 2025

2005 column:

1
1
18
15
39
270
TOTAL RENEWABLE ENERGY **343**

TOTAL NUCLEAR AND OTHER SOURCES **932**

782

150

TOTAL FOSSIL FUELS **2,780**

1,977

627

176

2030 — Assuming Current Trends:

26 41
251
92
139
314
TOTAL 864

TOTAL 926

824

102

TOTAL 3,358

2,567

647

144

2030 — Assuming 25% Renewables by 2025:

65   SOLAR PHOTOVOLTAIC
143 CONCENTRATING SOLAR
531 WIND
82   GEOTHERMAL
139 BIOMASS
314 HYDRO
TOTAL **1,275**

TOTAL **921**
824 NUCLEAR
96   OTHER

TOTAL **3,020**
2,383 COAL
512 NATURAL GAS
126 COGENERATION

RENEWABLE FUTURES

Under current policies, solar energy is projected to supply just over one percent of U.S. electricity by 2030 (middle bar). If demand for electricity rises, so will fossil fuel use—and carbon emissions. Requiring utilities to generate 25 percent of their power from renewable sources (right bar) would limit the growth of fossil fuels while pushing solar to 4 percent and wind to more than 10 percent of the total. Such forecasts are highly uncertain; policies and markets can both evolve in unforeseen ways.

*PROJECTIONS BASED ON 2005 DATA
**INCLUDES NONBIOGENIC MUNICIPAL WASTE, REFINERY GAS, AND OTHER SOURCES

NOTE: NUMBERS MAY NOT ADD UP TO TOTAL BECAUSE OF ROUNDING.

CHART BY 5W INFOGRAPHICS
SOURCE: UNION OF CONCERNED SCIENTISTS

probably remain a minor contributor (chart). Cap-and-trade legislation that sets a price on carbon emissions would not be a magic bullet for solar either. Both mandates would likely lead utilities to favor the cheapest renewables, like wind. Solar would make a sizable contribution only after 2025, once the expansion of wind energy had plateaued.

Some advocates say we need to encourage solar more directly. European nations have done so with "feed-in tariffs," laws that require electric utilities to pay premiums to solar-power producers, be they commercial power plants or private homes that pump energy to the grid. Such tariffs have made Germany and Spain solar leaders, creating a market that has helped drive down prices. The billions of dollars of tax credits and loan guarantees in the Obama stimulus package may have a similar effect.

Another option is for the federal government to invest directly in solar—for example, says Ken Zweibel of George Washington University, by funding the construction of giant solar plants in the desert Southwest, along with the high-efficiency transmission lines needed to carry the power nationwide. In Zweibel's version of the future, the sun would satisfy more than two-thirds of U.S. electricity needs by 2050, for an investment of about $400 billion. "Compared to what we just paid for the financial bailout, it's pocket change," he says. —Chris Carroll

Discussion Questions

- What is Achenbach's purpose in this article, and where does his purpose become especially clear?

- What are the most surprising pieces of information that he presents?

- What is "electrical intelligence," and how does it relate to the ways we use energy today?

- How did the Northeastern blackout of 2003 demonstrate our grid's vulnerabilities, and what lessons were learned from it?

Writing Activities

- In what ways do conflicts between the goals of the utility industry and interests in developing renewable energy work against progress toward cleaner methods of producing and transmitting energy in this country? In your view, is there enough incentive to "fix the infrastructure," or not? Provide clear and well-developed reasons to support your view.

- Read "Can Solar Save Us?" and examine this short piece as it relates to the more detailed picture Achenbach paints of our energy needs and the current state of our infrastructure. Consider this question: How likely is the United States to make significant strides in developing renewable energy in your lifetime? Zweibel estimates that we would need to invest $400 billion to enable solar energy to become the source for "more than two-thirds of U.S. electricity needs by 2050" (128). Based on your understanding of our political and economic challenges, will we take the steps necessary to achieve that goal? Support your view with well-chosen examples from the two readings and from your own experience.

- Interview at least three people from your family, your community, or your academic institution. Assess their energy awareness. Find out whether they would be willing to pay slightly higher utility rates in return for seeing how much they are spending on energy at different times of day. Would they be willing to pay more to have more control over their electricity use? Present their responses and your analysis in an essay that examines Americans' awareness of their energy use and their willingness to change based on increased awareness.

- Does Joel Achenbach's article answer the question his article opens with: "Can we fix the infrastructure that powers our lives?" Write an essay that analyzes the problem and the solutions as he sees them, with a focus on the answer to the opening question, from Achenbach's perspective. Conclude with a paragraph that offers your own perspective of the picture Achenbach presents.

Collaborative Activities

- In what ways does the average American's awareness of electricity use need an "upgrade?" In a small group, discuss each member's views on whether or not the way we, as "creatures of the grid," think about our own habits can help change the way we use the grid. Go beyond that to discuss the role awareness plays in advancing our "electrical intelligence." What factors are most likely to lead us to developing cleaner sources of electricity and more efficient methods of distributing it?

- Who is responsible for the condition of the nation's grid today and whether or not it will meet the needs of the future? Does Achenbach provide any clues in his article? With a partner or two, find places in his essay that indicate how decisions about the grid have been made. Together, suggest where individuals can contribute to a better system in the future and where larger institutions are required to make the necessary changes.

SAVING ENERGY: IT STARTS AT HOME

Author Peter Miller and his wife PJ's ambitious month-long project to find out whether they could make a significant cut in their household "carbon diet" leads Miller to examine how energy can be made more efficient at home and beyond, with minimal cost, and what challenges lie ahead in significantly lowering carbon emissions on a broader scale.

As you read "Saving Energy: It Starts at Home," consider the following questions:

- How feasible is it for individual households to cut carbon emissions by Miller's target of 80%, and what would be gained by making less drastic cuts?
- To what extent does the author's experiment provide an incentive for individuals to make lifestyle changes similar to the ones he and his wife made?
- How do Americans' carbon emissions compare with those of Europeans and the rest of the world, and what are the reasons for discrepancies among them?
- What sources of carbon emissions seem the easiest to control, and why isn't more being done to facilitate energy conservation in those areas?

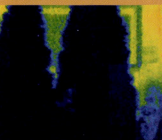

Thermographic photography offers clues to where energy is being wasted in this older house in Connecticut. Red and yellow patches indicate escaping heat, while new double-pane windows appear cool blue. By sealing in warmth, the windows cut heating costs, which can account for up to half a family's energy bill.

SAVING ENERGY:
IT STARTS
AT HOME

Photographs by Tyrone Turner

THE MISSING POWER PLANT

Instead of building a new 730-megawatt facility like the Decker Power Plant, the Austin, Texas, electric utility reduced demand by the same amount through rebates on energy-saving appliances and other programs. "Go into any store in Austin, and you can't buy an inefficient air conditioner," says general manager Roger Duncan. "They just stopped stocking them."

WE ALREADY KNOW THE FASTEST, LEAST EXPENSIVE WAY TO SLOW CLIMATE CHANGE: USE LESS ENERGY.

WITH A LITTLE EFFORT, AND NOT MUCH MONEY,

MOST OF US COULD REDUCE OUR ENERGY DIETS BY 25 PERCENT OR MORE—DOING THE EARTH A FAVOR WHILE ALSO HELPING OUR POCKETBOOKS. SO WHAT'S HOLDING US BACK?

Not long ago, my wife, PJ, and I tried a new diet—not to lose a little weight but to answer a nagging question about climate change. Scientists have reported recently that the world is heating up even faster than predicted only a few years ago, and that the consequences could be severe if we don't keep reducing emissions of carbon dioxide and other greenhouse gases that are trapping heat in our atmosphere. But what can we do about it as individuals? And as emissions from China, India, and other developing nations skyrocket, will our efforts really make any difference?

We decided to try an experiment. For one month we tracked our personal emissions of carbon dioxide (CO_2) as if we were counting calories. We wanted to see how much we could cut back, so we put ourselves on a strict diet. The average U.S. household produces about 150 pounds of CO_2 a day by doing commonplace things like turning on air-conditioning or driving cars. That's more than twice the European average and almost five times the global average, mostly because Americans

To stay below that threshold, we need to reduce CO_2 emissions by 80 percent.

drive more and have bigger houses. But how much should we try to reduce?

For an answer, I checked with Tim Flannery, author of *The Weather Makers: How Man Is Changing the Climate and What It Means for Life on Earth.* In his book, he'd challenged readers to make deep cuts in personal emissions to keep the world from reaching critical tipping points, such as the melting of the ice sheets in Greenland or West Antarctica. "To stay below that threshold, we need to reduce CO_2 emissions by 80 percent," he said.

"That sounds like a lot," PJ said. "Can we really do that?"

It seemed unlikely to me too. Still, the point was to answer a simple question: How close could we come to a lifestyle the planet could handle? If it turned out we couldn't do it, perhaps we could at least identify places where the diet pinched and figure out ways to adjust. So

Adapted from "Saving Energy: It Starts at Home" by Peter Miller: National Geographic Magazine, March 2009.

we agreed to shoot for 80 percent less than the U.S. average, which equated to a daily diet of only 30 pounds of CO_2. Then we set out to find a few neighbors to join us.

John and Kyoko Bauer were logical candidates. Dedicated greenies, they were already committed to a low-impact lifestyle. One car, one TV, no meat except fish. As parents of three-year-old twins, they were also worried about the future. "Absolutely, sign us up," John said.

Susan and Mitch Freedman, meanwhile, had two teenagers. Susan wasn't sure how eager they would be to cut back during their summer vacation, but she was game to give the diet a try. As an architect, Mitch was working on an office building designed to be energy efficient, so he was curious how much they could save at home. So the Freedmans were in too.

We started on a sunday in July, an unseasonably mild day in Northern Virginia, where we live. A front had blown through the night before, and I'd opened our bedroom windows to let in the breeze. We'd gotten so used to keeping our air-conditioning going around the clock, I'd almost forgotten the windows even opened. The birds woke us at five with a pleasant racket in the trees, the sun came up, and our experiment began.

Our first challenge was to find ways to convert our daily activities into pounds of CO_2. We wanted to track our progress as we went, to change our habits if necessary.

PJ volunteered to read our electric meter each morning and to check the odometer on our Mazda Miata. While she was doing that, I wrote down the mileage from our Honda CR-V and pushed my way through the shrubs to read the natural gas meter. We diligently recorded everything on a chart taped to one of our kitchen cabinets. A gallon of gasoline, we learned, adds a whopping 19.6 pounds of

If we turned off home computers when not in use, we would cut their CO_2 impact by 8.3 million tons a year, or 50 percent.

CO_2 to the atmosphere, a big chunk of our daily allowance. A kilowatt-hour (kWh) of electricity in the U.S. produces 1.5 pounds of CO_2. Every 100 cubic feet of natural gas emits 12 pounds of CO_2.

To get a rough idea of our current carbon footprint, I plugged numbers from recent utility bills into several calculators on websites. Each asked for slightly different information, and each came up with a different result. None was flattering. The Environmental Protection Agency (EPA) website figured our annual CO_2 emissions at 54,273 pounds, 30 percent higher than the average American family with two people; the main culprit was the energy we were using to heat and cool our house. Evidently, we had further to go than I thought.

I began our campaign by grabbing a flashlight and heading down to the basement. For most families, the water heater alone consumes 12 percent of their house's energy. My plan was to turn down the heater's thermostat to 120°F, as experts recommend. But taking a close look at our tank, I saw only "hot" and "warm" settings, no degrees. Not knowing what that meant exactly, I twisted the dial to warm and hoped for the best. (The water turned out to be a little cool, and I had to adjust it later.)

When PJ drove off in the CR-V to pick up a friend for church, I hauled out gear to cut the grass: electric lawn mower, electric edger, electric leaf blower. Then it dawned on me: All this power-sucking equipment was going to cost us in CO_2 emissions. So I stuffed everything back into the garage, hopped in the Miata, and buzzed down the street to Home Depot to price out an old-fashioned push reel mower.

The store didn't have one, so I drove a few miles more to Lawn & Leisure, an outfit that specializes in lawn mowers. They were out too, though they had plenty of big riding mowers on display. (The average gasoline-powered push mower, I'd learned, puts out as much pollution per hour as eleven cars—a riding mower as much as 34 cars.) My next stop was Wal-Mart, where I found another empty spot on the rack. I finally tried Sears, which had one manual mower left, the display model.

I'd seen advertisements for the latest reel mowers that made them sound like precision instruments, not the clunky beast I pushed as a teenager. But when I gave the display model a spin across the sales floor, I was disappointed. The reel felt clumsy compared with my corded electric model, which I can easily maneuver with one hand. I got back in the car emptyhanded and drove home.

As I pulled into the driveway, I had the sinking realization I'd been off on a fool's errand. I didn't know exactly how foolish until the next morning, when we added up the numbers. I'd driven 24 miles in search of a more Earth-friendly mower. PJ had driven 27 miles to visit a friend in an assisted-living facility. We'd used 32 kWh of electricity and 100 cubic feet of gas to cook dinner and dry our clothes. Our total CO_2 emissions for the day: 105.6 pounds. Three and a half times our target.

"Guess we need to try harder," PJ said.

We got some help in week two from a professional "house doctor," Ed Minch, of Energy Services Group in Wilmington, Delaware. We asked Minch to do an energy audit of our house to see if we'd missed any easy fixes. The first thing he did was walk around the outside of the house, looking at how the "envelope" was put together. Had the architect and builder created any opportunities for air to seep in or out, such as overhanging floors? Next he went inside and used an infrared scanner to look at our interior walls. A hot or cold spot might mean that we had a duct problem or that insulation in a wall wasn't doing its job. Finally his assistants set up a powerful fan in our front door to lower air pressure inside the house and force air through whatever leaks there might be in the shell of the house. Our house, his instruments showed, was 50 percent leakier than it should be.

Minch also gave us tips about lighting and appliances. "A typical kitchen these days has ten 75-watt spots on all day," he said. "That's a huge waste of money." Replacing them with compact fluorescents could save a homeowner $200 a year. Refrigerators, washing machines, dishwashers, and other appliances, in fact, may represent half of a household's electric bill. Those with Energy Star labels from the EPA are more efficient and may come with rebates or tax credits when you buy them, Minch said.

There was no shortage of advice out there, I discovered, about ways to cut back on CO_2 emissions. Even before Minch's visit, I'd collected stacks of printouts and brochures from environmental websites and utility companies. In a sense, there's almost too much information.

"You can't fix everything at once," John Bauer said when I asked how he and Kyoko were getting along. "When we became vegetarians, we didn't do it all at once. First the lamb went. Then the pork. Then the beef. Finally the chicken. We've been phasing out seafood for a few years now. It's no different with a carbon diet."

Good advice, I'm sure. But everywhere I looked I saw things gobbling up energy. One night I sat up in bed, squinted into the darkness, and counted ten little lights: cell phone charger, desktop calculator, laptop computer, printer, clock radio, cable TV box, camera battery recharger, carbon monoxide detector, cordless phone base, smoke detector. What were they all doing? A study by the Lawrence Berkeley National Laboratory found that "vampire" power sucked up by electronics in standby mode can add up to 8 percent of a house's electric bill. What else had I missed? (Continued on page 138)

BRINGING THE FARM TO THE CITY

If tomatoes, cucumbers, lettuce, strawberries, pumpkins, and other crops can grow on a barge in the Hudson River, then why not on New Yourk City rooftops? That was the idea behind the Science Barge, a prototype of a carbon-neutral hydroponic farm that saves energy by eliminating the need for transportation.

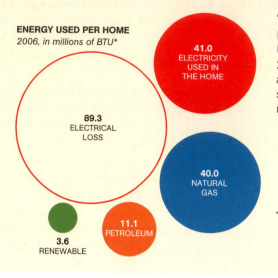

ENERGY USED PER HOME
2006, in millions of BTU*

41.0
ELECTRICITY
USED IN
THE HOME

89.3
ELECTRICAL
LOSS

40.0
NATURAL
GAS

11.1
PETROLEUM

3.6
RENEWABLE

THE POWERED HOUSE

Electricity is the biggest source of power for U.S. homes—and for every kilowatt-hour used, 2.2 are "lost" as that energy is generated and sent over transmission lines. So, even small changes in our habits can scale up to big reductions in carbon emissions.

CO_2 AMOUNTS MEASURED IN METRIC TONS

* THE BRITISH THERMAL UNIT (BTU) IS USED TO MEASURE THE ENERGY CONTENT OF FUELS AND THE POWER OF HEATING AND COOLING SYSTEMS. ONE KILOWATT-HOUR OF ELECTRICITY IS EQUIVALENT TO 3,412 BTU.

SEAN MCNAUGHTON, NG STAFF

SOURCE: ENERGY INFORMATION ADMINISTRATION, *ANNUAL ENERGY OUTLOOK 2008*

(Continued from page 135) At this point we left home for a long weekend to attend the wedding of my niece, Alyssa, in Oregon. While we were gone, the house sitter caring for our two dogs continued to read our gas and electric meters, and we kept track of the mileage on our rental car as we drove from Portland to the Pacific coast. I knew this trip wasn't going to help our carbon diet any. But what was more important, after all, reducing CO_2 emissions or sharing a family celebration?

That's the big question. How significant are personal efforts to cut back? Do our actions add up to anything meaningful, or are we just making ourselves feel better? I still wasn't sure. As soon as we returned home to Virginia, I started digging up more numbers.

The United States, I learned, produces a fifth of the world's CO_2 emissions, about six billion metric tons a year. That staggering amount could reach seven billion by 2030, as our population and economy continue to grow. Most of the CO_2 comes from energy consumed by buildings, vehicles, and industries. How much CO_2 could be avoided,

I started to wonder, if we all tightened our belts? What would happen if the whole country went on a carbon diet?

Buildings, not cars, produce the most CO_2 in the United States. Private residences, shopping malls, warehouses, and offices account for 38 percent of the nation's emissions, mainly because of electricity use. It doesn't help that the average new house in the United States is 45 percent bigger than it was 30 years ago.

Companies like Wal-Mart that maintain thousands of their own buildings have discovered they can achieve significant energy savings. A pilot Supercenter in Las Vegas consumes up to 45 percent less power than similar stores, in part by using evaporative cooling units, radiant floors, high-efficiency refrigeration, and natural light in shopping areas. Retrofits and smart design could reduce emissions from buildings in this country by 200 million tons of CO_2 a year, according to researchers at Oak Ridge National Laboratory. But Americans are unlikely to achieve such gains, they say, without new building codes, appliance standards, and financial incentives. There are simply too many reasons not to.

Commercial building owners, for example, have had little incentive to pay more for improvements like high-efficiency windows, lights, heating, or cooling systems since their tenants, not they, pay the energy bills, said Harvey Sachs of the American Council for an Energy-Efficient Economy. For homeowners, meanwhile, efficiency takes a backseat whenever money is tight. In a 2007 survey of Americans, 60 percent said they didn't have enough savings to pay for energy-related renovations. If given anextra $10,000 to work with, only 24 percent said they would invest in efficiency. What did the rest want? Granite countertops.

After buildings, transportation is the next largest source of CO_2, producing 34 percent of the nation's emissions. Carmakers have been told by Congress to raise fuel economy standards by 40 percent by 2020. But emissions will still grow, because the number of miles driven in this country keeps going up. One big reason: Developers keep pushing neighborhoods farther into the countryside, making it unavoidable for families to spend hours a day in their cars. An EPA study estimated that greenhouse gas emissions from vehicles could increase 80 percent over the next 50 years. Unless we make it easier for Americans to choose buses, subways, and bikes over cars, experts say, there's little chance for big emissions cuts from vehicles.

The industrial sector represents the third major source of CO_2. Refineries, paper plants, and other facilities emit 28 percent of the nation's total. You would think such enterprises would have eliminated

> **I**f we improved our cars' gas mileage by 5 miles a gallon, we could **cut their CO_2 emissions by 239 million tons each year, a 20 percent decrease.**

inefficiencies long ago. But that isn't always the case. For firms competing in global markets, making the best product at the right price comes first. Reducing greenhouse gases is less urgent. Some don't even track CO_2 emissions.

A number of corporations such as Dow, DuPont, and 3M have shown how profitable efficiency can be. Since 1995, Dow has saved seven billion dollars by reducing its energy intensity—the amount of energy consumed per pound of product—and during the past few decades it has cut its CO_2 emissions by 20 percent. To show other companies how to make such gains, the Department of Energy (DOE) has been sending teams of experts into 700 or so factories a year to analyze equipment and techniques. Yet even here change doesn't come easily. Managers are reluctant to invest in efficiency unless the return is high and the payback time is short. Even when tips from the experts involve no cost at all—such as "turn off the ventilation in unoccupied rooms"—fewer than half of such fixes are acted upon. One reason is inertia. "Many changes don't happen until the maintenance foreman, who knows how to keep the old equipment running, dies or retires," said Peggy Podolak, senior industrial energy analyst at DOE.

But change is coming anyway. Most business leaders expect federal regulation of CO_2 emissions in the near future. Already, New York and nine other northeastern states have agreed on a mandatory cap-and-trade system similar to the one started in Europe in 2005. Under the plan, launched last year, emissions from large power plants will be reduced over time, as each plant either cuts emissions or purchases credits from other companies that

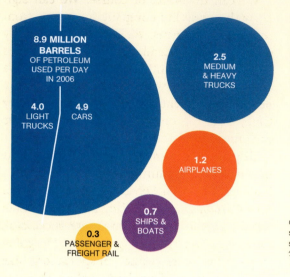

TRANSPORTATION TOLLS

Cars and light trucks consume the lion's share of petroleum used for transportation in the United States. Modest changes in efficiency and driving habits could add up to significant fuel savings.

8.9 MILLION BARRELS OF PETROLEUM USED PER DAY IN 2006

4.0 LIGHT TRUCKS

4.9 CARS

2.5 MEDIUM & HEAVY TRUCKS

1.2 AIRPLANES

0.7 SHIPS & BOATS

0.3 PASSENGER & FREIGHT RAIL

CO₂ AMOUNTS MEASURED IN METRIC TONS

SEAN MCNAUGHTON, NG STAFF

SOURCES: ENERGY INFORMATION ADMINISTRATION, *ANNUAL ENERGY OUTLOOK 2008*; DEPARTMENT OF ENERGY, *TRANSPORTATION ENERGY DATA BOOK, EDITION 27*

cut their emissions. A similar scheme has been launched by the governors of California and six other western states and the premiers of four Canadian provinces.

So how do the numbers add up? How much CO_2 could we save if the whole nation went on a low carbon diet? A study by McKinsey & Company, a management consulting firm, estimated that the United States could avoid 1.3 billion tons of CO_2 emissions a year, using only existing technologies that would pay for themselves in savings. Instead of growing by more than a billion tons by 2020, annual emissions in the U.S. would drop by 200 million tons a year. We already know, in other words, how to freeze CO_2 emissions if we want to.

Not that there won't still be obstacles. Every sector of our economy faces challenges, said energy-efficiency guru Amory Lovins of the Rocky Mountain Institute. "But they all have huge potential. I don't know anyone who has failed to make money at energy efficiency. There's so much low-hanging fruit, it's falling off the trees and mushing up around our ankles."

By the last week in july, PJ and I were finally getting into the flow of the reduced carbon lifestyle. We walked to the neighborhood pool instead of driving, biked to the farmers market on Saturday morning, and lingered on the deck until dark, chatting over the chirping of the crickets. Whenever possible I worked from home, and when I commuted I took the bus and subway. Even when it got hot and humid, as it does in Virginia in July, we were never really uncomfortable, thanks in part to the industrial-size ceiling fan we installed in the bedroom in late June.

"That fan's my new best friend," PJ said.

Our numbers were looking pretty good, in fact, when we crossed the finish line on August 1. Compared with the previous July, we slashed electricity use by 70 percent, natural gas by 40 percent, and reduced our driving to half the national average. In terms of CO_2, we trimmed our emissions to an average of 70.5 pounds a day, which, though twice as much as we'd targeted as our goal, was still half the national average.

These were encouraging results, I thought, until I factored in emissions from our plane trip to Oregon. I hadn't expected that a modern aircraft packed with passengers would emit almost half as much CO_2 per person as PJ and I would have produced if we'd driven to Oregon and back in the CR-V. The round-trip flight added the equivalent of 2,500 pounds of CO_2 to our bottom line, more than doubling our daily average from 70.5 pounds of CO_2 to 150 pounds—five times our goal. So much for air travel.

By comparison, the Bauers did significantly better, though they also faced setbacks. Since their house is all electric, Kyoko Bauer had tried to reduce her use of the clothes dryer by hanging laundry on a rack outside, as she and John had done when they lived in arid Western Australia. But with their busy three-year-olds, Etienne and Ajanta, she was doing as many as 14 loads a week, and it took all day for clothes to dry in Virginia's humid air. "It wasn't as convenient as I hoped," she said. "I had to race home from shopping a couple of times before it started to rain." Their bottom line: 97.4 pounds of CO_2 a day.

For the Freedmans, driving turned out to be the big bump in the road. With four cars and everyone commuting to a job every day—including Ben and Courtney—they racked up 4,536 miles during the month. "I don't know how we could have driven less," Susan said. "We were all going in different directions and there wasn't any other way to get there." Their bottom line: 248 pounds of CO_2 a day.

When we received our electric bill for July, PJ and I were pleased that our efforts had saved us $190. We decided to use a portion of this windfall to offset the airline emissions. After doing a little homework, we contributed $50 to Native Energy, one of many companies and nonprofits that save CO_2 by investing in wind farms, solar plants, and other renewable energy projects. Our purchase was enough to counteract a ton of jet emissions, roughly what we added through our trip and then some.

We can do more, of course. We can sign up with our utility company for power from regional wind farms. We can purchase locally grown foods instead of winter raspberries from Chile and bottled water from Fiji. We can join a carbon-reduction club through a neighborhood church, Scout troop, Rotary Club, PTA, or environmental group. If we can't find one, we could start one.

"If you can get enough people to do things in enough communities, you can have a huge impact," said David Gershon, author of *Low Carbon Diet: A 30-Day Program to Lose 5,000 Pounds.* "When people are successful, they say, Wow, I want to go further. I'm going to push for better public transportation, bike lanes, whatever. Somebody called this the mice-on-the-ice strategy. You don't have to get any one element to work, but if you come at it from enough different directions, eventually the ice cracks."

Will it make any difference? That's what we really wanted to know. Our low carbon diet had shown us that, with little or no hardship and no major cash outlays, we could cut day-to-day emissions of CO_2 in half—mainly by wasting less energy at home and on the highway. Similar efforts in office buildings, shopping malls, and factories throughout the nation, combined with incentives and effiiency standards, could halt further increases in U.S. emissions.

That won't be enough by itself, though. The world will still suffer severe disruptions unless humanity reduces emissions sharply—and they've risen 30 percent since 1990. As much as 80 percent of new energy demand in the next decade is projected to come from China, India, and other developing nations. China is building the equivalent of two midsize coal-fired power plants a week, and by 2007 its CO_2 output surpassed that of the United States Putting the brakes on global emissions will be more difficult than curbing CO_2 in the United States, because the economies of developing nations are growing faster.

But it begins the same way: By focusing on better insulation in houses, more efficient lights in offices, better gas mileage in cars, and smarter processes in industry. The potential exists, as McKinsey reported last year, to cut the growth of global emissions in half. Yet efficiency, in the end, can only take us so far. To get the deeper reductions we need, as Tim Flannery advised—80 percent by 2050 (or even 100 percent, as he now advocates)—we must replace fossil fuels faster with renewable energy from wind farms, solar plants, geothermal facilities, and biofuels. We must slow deforestation, which is an additional source of greenhouse gases. And we must develop technologies to capture and bury carbon dioxide from existing power plants.

Efficiency can buy us time—perhaps as much as two decades—to figure out how to remove carbon from the world's diet.

The rest of the world isn't waiting for the United States to show the way. Sweden has pioneered carbon-neutral houses, Germany affordable solar power, Japan fuel-efficient cars, the Netherlands prosperous cities filled with bicycles. Do Americans have the will to match such efforts?

This movement starts at home with the changing of a lightbulb, the opening of a window, a walk to the bus, or a bike ride to the post office. PJ and I did it for only a month, but I can see the low carbon diet becoming a habit.

"What do we have to lose?" PJ said.

Discussion Questions

- Do Peter and his wife represent typical Americans? Why or why not?

- How does Miller's breakdown of his family's carbon footprint help you understand your and your household's footprint? What similarities or differences stand out to you?

- How compelling are the reasons not to reduce emissions in business sector compared with incentives to do it? Why are there so few examples of successful energy saving efforts to report?

- What would Miller say we stand to gain from asking the question, "what would happen if the whole country went on a carbon diet" (138)?

Writing Activities

- Does Miller's experiment convince you that "Americans have the will to match [Sweden, Germany, Japan, and the Netherlands'] efforts" to drastically reduce carbon emissions? If we possess the will, why are we not making more progress? If we lack it, what are the reasons for our inability to take more decisive action in the face of a crisis? Write an essay that analyzes Americans' attitudes about reducing global carbon emissions and offer some insight into our behavior as it relates to energy use.

- Miller suggests that eliminating waste is a key factor in reducing carbon emissions in business and industry, yet little is done to reduce energy waste or inefficiency. Write an essay that proposes some ways to reduce "inertia" and motivate companies to take steps to save money as well as reduce emissions.

- Considering some of Miller's examples and your own observations, does his essay provide a satisfying answer to the question it poses? Explain why or why not.

- Write a persuasive essay that explains how you see the U.S.'s role in fighting global climate change and offers suggestions about how we might step forward as individuals to strengthen our sense of responsibility and change our lifestyles in order to reduce our carbon footprint.

Collaborative Activities

- Following Miller's breakdown of the U.S.'s primary carbon emissions sources into categories, discuss with a small group the changes in each area that would most significantly lower emissions and the biggest challenges standing in the way of such changes.

- Has your college/university taken any steps to save energy? Working in pairs, interview an administrator, buildings and grounds staff, a member of student government, and/or an instructor in a related field to determine how your campus rates in terms of energy savings. Inquire about low-cost steps that your academic institution could take to make improvements. Present your findings to the class.

HIGH-TECH TRASH

Chris Carroll's article sheds light on a problem that is hidden from the average American or European's view, despite its size. Our throwaway culture, combined with the short life-span of our electronic devices and a system that encourages the export of highly toxic e-waste to developing countries, has resulted in a large-scale market in those nations who—legally or illegally—accept and reuse or resell the components of our toxic trash.

As you read "High-Tech Trash," consider the following questions:

- What factors contribute to the market for e-waste in developing countries?
- Why is so little e-waste recycled by the nations of the developed world?
- In what ways have efforts to regulate high-tech trash failed in Europe and the United States?
- What hope do new business models offer for safer alternatives to shipping toxic e-waste overseas, and what steps must be taken in order to create viable alternatives?

HIGH-TECH TRASH

Photographs by Peter Essick

A boy totes copper wires torn from old electronic devices at a market in Ghana. Power plugs in his bundle point to Europe—where laws forbid shipping such waste to poor nations—as a likely origin.

WILL YOUR DISCARDED
TV OR COMPUTER
END UP IN A DITCH IN GHANA?

June is the wet season in Ghana, but here in Accra, the capital, the morning rain has ceased. As the sun heats the humid air, pillars of black smoke begin to rise above the vast Agbogbloshie Market. I follow one plume toward its source, past lettuce and plantain vendors, past stalls of used tires, and through a clanging scrap market where hunched men bash on old alternators and engine blocks. Soon the muddy track is flanked by piles of old TVs, gutted computer cases, and smashed monitors heaped ten feet high. Beyond lies a field of fine ash speckled with glints of amber and green—the sharp broken bits of circuit boards. I can see now that the smoke issues not from one fire, but from many small blazes. Dozens of indistinct figures move among the acrid haze, some stirring flames with sticks, others carrying armfuls of brightly colored computer wire. Most are children.

Choking, I pull my shirt over my nose and approach a boy of about 15, his thin frame

Future archaeologists will note that at the tail end of the 20th century, a new, noxious kind of clutter exploded across the landscape: the digital detritus that has come to be called e-waste.

wreathed in smoke. Karim says he has been tending such fires for two years. He pokes at one meditatively, and then his top half disappears as he bends into the billowing soot. He hoists a tangle of copper wire off the old tire he's using for fuel and douses the hissing mass in a puddle. With the flame retardant insulation burned away—a process that has released a bouquet of carcinogens and other toxics—the wire may fetch a dollar from a scrap-metal buyer.

Another day in the market, on a similar ash heap above an inlet that flushes to the Atlantic after a downpour, Israel Mensah, an incongruously stylish young man of about 20, adjusts his designer glasses and explains how he makes his living. Each day scrap sellers bring loads of old electronics—from where he doesn't know. Mensah and his partners—friends and family, including two shoeless boys raptly listening to us talk—buy a

Adapted from "High-Tech Trash" by Chris Carroll: National Geographic Magazine, January 2008.

few computers or TVs. They break copper yokes off picture tubes, littering the ground with shards containing lead, a neurotoxin, and cadmium, a carcinogen that damages lungs and kidneys. They strip resalable parts such as drives and memory chips. Then they rip out wiring and burn the plastic. He sells copper stripped from one scrap load to buy another. The key to making money is speed, not safety. "The gas goes to your nose and you feel something in your head," Mensah says, knocking his fist against the back of his skull for effect. "Then you get sick in your head and your chest." Nearby, hulls of broken monitors float in the lagoon. Tomorrow the rain will wash them into the ocean. People have always been proficient at making trash. Future archaeologists will note that at the tail end of the 20th century, a new, noxious kind of clutter exploded across the landscape: the digital detritus that has come to be called e-waste.

More than 40 years ago, Gordon Moore, co-founder of the computer-chip maker Intel, observed that computer processing power roughly doubles every two years. An unstated corollary to "Moore's law" is that at any given time, all the machines considered state-of-the-art are simultaneously on the verge of obsolescence. At this very moment, heavily caffeinated software engineers are designing programs that will overtax and befuddle your new turbo-powered PC when you try running them a few years from now. The memory and graphics requirements of Microsoft's recent Vista operating system, for instance, spell doom for aging machines that were still able to squeak by a year ago. According to the U.S. Environmental Protection Agency, an estimated 30 to 40 million PCs will be ready for "end-of-life management" in each of the next few years.

Computers are hardly the only electronic hardware hounded by obsolescence. A switchover to digital high-definition television broadcasts is scheduled to be complete by 2009,

> **A**n unstated corollary to "Moore's law" is that at any given time, all the machines considered state-of-theart **are simultaneously on the verge of obsolescence.**

rendering inoperable TVs that function perfectly today but receive only an analog signal. As viewers prepare for the switch, about 25 million TVs are taken out of service yearly. In the fashion-conscious mobile market, 98 million U.S. cell phones took their last call in 2005. All told, the EPA estimates that in the United States that year, between 1.5 and 1.9 million tons of computers, TVs, VCRs, monitors, cell phones, and other equipment were discarded. If all sources of electronic waste are tallied, it could total 50 million tons a year worldwide, according to the UN Environment Programme.

So what happens to all this junk?

In the United States, it is estimated that more than 70 percent of discarded computers and monitors, and well over 80 percent of TVs, eventually end up in landfills, despite a growing number of state laws that prohibit dumping of e-waste, which may leak lead, mercury, arsenic, cadmium, beryllium, and other toxics into the ground. Meanwhile, a staggering volume of unused electronic gear sits in storage—about 180 million TVs, desktop PCs, and other components as of 2005, according to the EPA. Even if this obsolete equipment remains in attics and basements indefinitely, never reaching a landfill, this solution has its own, indirect impact on the environment. In addition to toxics, e-waste contains goodly amounts of silver, gold, and other valuable metals that are highly efficient conductors of electricity. In theory, recycling gold from old computer motherboards is far more efficient and less environmentally destructive than ripping it from the earth, often by surface-mining that imperils pristine rain forests.

Currently, less than 20 percent of e-waste entering the solid waste stream is channeled through companies that advertise themselves as recyclers, though the number is likely to rise as states like California crack down on landfill dumping. Yet recycling, under the current system, is less benign than it sounds. Dropping your old electronic gear off with a recycling company or at a municipal collection point does not guarantee that it will be safely disposed of. While some recyclers process the material with an eye toward minimizing pollution and health risks, many more sell it to brokers who ship it to the developing world, where environmental enforcement is weak. For people in countries on the front end of this arrangement, it's a handy out-of-sight, out-of-mind solution.

Many governments, conscious that electronic waste wrongly handled damages the environment and human health, have tried to weave an international regulatory net. The 1989 Basel Convention, a 170-nation accord, requires that developed nations notify developing nations of incoming hazardous waste shipments. Environmental groups and many undeveloped nations called the terms too weak, and in 1995 protests led to an amendment known as the Basel Ban, which forbids hazardous waste shipments to poor countries. Though the ban has yet to take effect, the European Union has written the requirements into its laws.

The EU also requires manufacturers to shoulder the burden of safe disposal. Recently a new EU directive encourages "green design" of electronics, setting limits for allowable levels of lead, mercury, fire retardants, and other substances. Another directive requires manufacturers to set up infrastructure to collect e-waste and ensure responsible recycling—a strategy called take-back. In spite of these safeguards, untold tons of e-waste still slip out of European ports, on their way to the developing world.

In the United States, electronic waste has been less of a legislative priority. One of only three countries to sign but not ratify the Basel Convention (the other two are Haiti and Afghanistan), it does not require green design or take-back programs of manufacturers, though a few states have stepped in with their own laws. The U.S. approach, says Matthew Hale, EPA solid waste program director, is instead to encourage responsible recycling by working with industry—for instance, with a ratings system that rewards environmentally sound products with a seal of approval. "We're definitely trying to channel market forces, and look for cooperative approaches and consensus standards," Hale says.

The result of the federal hands-off policy is that the greater part of e-waste sent to domestic recyclers is shunted overseas.

"We in the developed world get the benefit from these devices," says Jim Puckett, head of Basel Action Network, or BAN, a group that opposes hazardous waste shipments to developing nations. "But when our equipment becomes unusable, we externalize the real environmental costs and liabilities to the developing world."

Asia is the center of much of the world's high-tech manufacturing, and it is here the devices often return when they die. China in particular has long been the world's electronics graveyard. With explosive growth in its manufacturing sector fueling demand, China's ports have become conduits for recyclable scrap of every sort: steel, aluminum, plastic, even paper. By the mid-1980s, electronic waste began freely pouring into China as well, carrying the lucrative promise of the precious metals embedded in circuit boards.

China had specifically prohibited the import of electronic waste in 2000, but that had not stopped the trade. After the worldwide publicity BAN's film generated, however, the government lengthened the list of forbidden e-wastes and began pushing local governments to enforce the ban in earnest.

On a recent trip to Taizhou, a city in Zhejiang Province south of Shanghai that was another center of e-waste processing, I saw evidence of both the crackdown and its limits. Until a few years ago, the hill country outside Taizhou was the center of a huge but informal electronics disassembly industry that rivaled Guiyu's. But these days, customs officials at the nearby Haimen and Ningbo ports—clearinghouses for massive volumes of metal scrap—are sniffing around incoming shipments for illegal hazardous waste.

Today the salvagers operate in the shadows. Inside the open door of a house in a hillside village, a homeowner uses pliers to rip microchips and metal parts off a computer motherboard. A buyer will burn these pieces to recover copper. The man won't reveal his name. "This business is illegal," he admits, offering a cigarette. In the same village, several men huddle inside a shed, heating circuit boards over a flame to extract metal. Outside the door lies a pile of scorched boards. In another village a few miles away, a woman stacks up bags of circuit boards in her house. She shoos my translator and me away. Continuing through the hills, I see people tearing apart car batteries, alternators, and high-voltage cable for recycling, and others hauling aluminum scrap to an aging smelter. But I find no one else working with electronics. In Taizhou, at least, the e-waste business seems to be waning.

Yet for some people it is likely too late; a cycle of disease or disability is already in motion. In a spate of studies released last year, Chinese scientists documented the environmental plight of Guiyu, the site of the original BAN film. The air near some electronics salvage operations that remain open contains the highest amounts of dioxin measured anywhere in the world. Soils are saturated with the chemical, a probable carcinogen that may disrupt endocrine and immune function. High levels of flame retardants called PBDEs—common in electronics, and potentially damaging to fetal development even at very low levels—turned up in the blood of the electronics workers. The high school teacher in Taizhou says his students found high levels of PBDEs in plants and animals. Humans were also tested, but he was not at liberty to discuss the results.

China may someday succeed in curtailing electronic waste imports. But e-waste flows like water. Shipments that a few years ago might have gone to ports in Guangdong or Zhejiang Provinces can easily be diverted to friendlier environs in Thailand, Pakistan, or elsewhere. "It doesn't help in a global sense for one place like China, or India, to become restrictive," says David N. Pellow, an ethnic studies professor at the University of California, San Diego, who studies electronic waste

In a global economy, out of sight will not stay out of mind for long.

from a social justice perspective. "The flow simply shifts as it takes the path of least resistance to the bottom."

It is next to impossible to gauge how much e-waste is still being smuggled into China, diverted to other parts of Asia, or—increasingly—dumped in West African countries like Ghana, Nigeria, and Ivory Coast. At ground level, however, one can pick out single threads from this global toxic tapestry and follow them back to their source.

In Accra, Mike Anane, a local environmental journalist, takes me down to the seaport. Guards block us at the gate. But some truck drivers at a nearby gas station point us toward a shipment facility just up the street, where they say computers are often unloaded. There, in a storage yard, locals are opening a shipping container from Germany. Shoes, clothes, and handbags pour out onto the tarmac. Among the clutter: some battered Pentium 2 and 3 computers and monitors with cracked cases and missing knobs, all sitting in the rain. A man hears us asking questions. "You want computers?" he asks. "How many containers?"

Near the port I enter a garage-like building with a sign over the door: "Importers of British Used Goods." Inside: more age-encrusted PCs, TVs, and audio components. According to the manager, the owner of the facility imports a 40-foot container every week. Working items go up for sale. Broken ones are sold for a pittance to scrap collectors.

All around the city, the sidewalks are choked with used electronics shops. In a suburb called Darkuman, a dim stall is stacked front to back with CRT monitors. These are valueless relics in wealthy countries, particularly hard to dispose of because of their high levels of lead and other toxics. Apparently no one wants them here, either. Some are monochrome, with tiny screens. Boys will soon be smashing them up in a scrap market.

A price tag on one of the monitors bears the label of a chain of Goodwill stores headquartered in Frederick, Maryland, a 45-minute drive from my house. A lot of people donate their old computers to charity organizations, believing they're

CHILD LABOR

In Karachi, Pakistan, Salman Aziz, 11, harvests bits of metal from computer mice. As the volume of electronic waste continues to grow worldwide, so does the need for humane and environmentally sound ways to recycle the wealth of raw materials inside it.

doing the right thing. I might well have done the same. I ask the proprietor of the shop where he got the monitors. He tells me his brother in Alexandria, Virginia, sent them. He sees no reason not to give me his brother's phone number.

When his brother Baah finally returns my calls, he turns out not to be some shady character trying to avoid the press, but a maintenance man in an apartment complex, working 15-hour days fixing toilets and lights. To make ends meet, he tells me, he works nights and weekends exporting used computers to Ghana through his brother. A Pentium 3 brings $150 in Accra, and he can sometimes buy the machines for less than $10 on Internet liquidation websites—he favors private ones, but the U.S. General Services Administration runs one as well. Or he buys bulk loads from charity stores. (Managers of the Goodwill store

whose monitor ended up in Ghana denied selling large quantities of computers to dealers.) Whatever the source, the profit margin on a working computer is substantial.

The catch: Nothing is guaranteed to work, and companies always try to unload junk. CRT monitors, though useless, are often part of the deal. Baah has neither time nor space to unpack and test his monthly loads. "You take it over there and half of them don't work," he says disgustedly. All you can do then is sell it to scrap people, he says. "What they do with it from that point, I don't know nothing about it."

Baah's little exporting business is just one trickle in the cataract of e-waste flowing out of the United States and the rest of the developed world. In the long run, the only way to prevent it from flooding Accra, Taizhou, or a hundred other places is to carve a new, more responsible direction for it to flow in. A Tampa, Florida, company called Creative Recycling Systems has already begun.

The key to the company's business model rumbles away at one end of a warehouse—a building-size machine operating not unlike an assembly line in reverse. "David" was what company president Jon Yob called the more than three-million-dollar investment in machines and processes when they were installed in 2006; Goliath is the towering stockpile of U.S. e-scrap. Today the machine's steel teeth are chomping up audio and video components. Vacuum pressure and filters capture dust from the process. "The air that comes out is cleaner than the ambient air in the building," vice president Joe Yob (Jon's brother) bellows over the roar. A conveyor belt transports material from the shredder through a series of sorting stations: vibrating screens of varying finenesses, magnets, a device to extract leaded glass, and an eddy current separator—akin to a reverse magnet, Yob says—that propels nonferrous metals like copper and aluminum into a bin, along with precious metals like gold, silver, and palladium. The most valuable product, shredded circuit boards, is shipped to a state-of-the-art smelter in Belgium specializing in precious-metals recycling. According to Yob, a four-foot-square box of the stuff can be worth as much as $10,000.

In Europe, where the recycling infrastructure is more developed, plant-size recycling machines like David are fairly common. So far, only three other U.S. companies have such equipment. David can handle some 150 million pounds of electronics a year; it wouldn't take many more machines like it to process the entire country's output of high-tech trash. But under current policies, pound for pound it is still more profitable to ship waste abroad than to process it safely at home. "We can't compete economically with people who do it wrong, who ship it overseas," Joe Yob says. Creative Recycling's investment in David thus represents a gamble—one that could pay off if the EPA institutes a certification process for recyclers that would define minimum standards for the industry. Companies that rely mainly on export would have difficulty meeting such standards. The EPA is exploring certification options.

Ultimately, shipping e-waste overseas may be no bargain even for the developed world. In 2006 Jeffrey Weidenhamer, a chemist at Ashland University in Ohio, bought some cheap, Chinese-made jewelry at a local dollar store for his class to analyze. That the jewelry contained high amounts of lead was distressing, but hardly a surprise; Chinese-made leaded jewelry is all too commonly marketed in the United States. More revealing were the amounts of copper and tin alloyed with the lead. As Weidenhamer and his colleague Michael Clement argued in a scientific paper published this past July, the proportions of these metals in some samples suggest their source was leaded solder used in the manufacture of electronic circuit boards.

"The U.S. right now is shipping large quantities of leaded materials to China, and China is the world's major manufacturing center," Weidenhamer says. "It's not all that surprising things are coming full circle and now we're getting contaminated products back." In a global economy, out of sight will not stay out of mind for long.

Discussion Questions

- If governments are, in fact, "conscious that electronic waste wrongly handled damages the environment and human health" (149), what factors make it possible for the developing world to end up bearing all the risk?

- What role has the United States taken in regulating its disposal of e-waste? What concerns are raised by Carroll's report regarding how we handle the liabilities associated with e-waste?

- How have recyclers' assumptions about selling scrap to brokers failed to account for where that scrap goes?

- Whose responsibility is it to track hazardous waste and to make sure salvagers do not "operate in the shadows?"

Writing Activities

- Write a creative narrative from your last cell phone or older computer's point of view, describing its likely journey from your municipal waste processing center to its ultimate destination.

- What are your community's guidelines on disposing of e-waste? Do some research on disposal procedures, and write an evaluation of how your community handles e-waste, taking into account how much or little your local officials know about where the material goes, whether or not brokers are involved, and if any tracking measures are in place. Based on what you learn, how would you rate your community's performance?

- Write a letter to your state representative or an entrepreneur, explaining the need for incentives to encourage other companies like Creative Recycling Systems to develop and expand in the United States.

- Write a proposal to your local school board or town administrator that outlines an education or action campaign that would inform students and other community members about the life cycle of e-waste and suggest ways to protect the developing world from our toxic trash.

Collaborative Activities

- To what extent can public awareness lead to more responsible handling of e-waste? In a small group, share your responses to the information Carroll presents in this article. Then discuss the role consumers play in the process and whether or not they have the power to change what happens to their discarded devices. Taking the ideas further, compare/contrast the consumer's role with that of the manufacturer.

- Working together, identify the ways the market invites "brokers who ship [e-waste] to the developing world where enforcement is weak" (149), and brainstorm a list of ways to discourage such activity.